WILD
Idaho

Help Us Keep This Guide Up to Date

Every effort has been made by the author and editors to make this guide as accurate and useful as possible. However, many things can change after a guide is published—trails are rerouted, regulations change, techniques evolve, facilities come under new management, etc.

We would love to hear from you concerning your experiences with this guide and how you feel it could be improved and kept up to date. While we may not be able to respond to all comments and suggestions, we'll take them to heart, and we'll also make certain to share them with the author. Please send your comments and suggestions to the following address:

The Globe Pequot Press
Reader Response/Editorial Department
P.O. Box 480
Guilford, CT 06437

Or you may e-mail us at:

editorial@globe-pequot.com

Thanks for your input, and happy travels!

Wild
Idaho

A Guide to More than Thirty Roadless Recreation Areas

by
Wendy Swope

FALCON ®

GUILFORD, CONNECTICUT
HELENA, MONTANA
AN IMPRINT OF THE GLOBE PEQUOT PRESS

A FALCON GUIDE ®

Maps by Bruce Grubbs © The Globe Pequot Press
All interior photos courtesy of Idaho Department of Commerce, except p. 117 photo courtesy of Rick Just, Idaho Department of Parks and Recreation.

Library of Congress Cataloging-in-Publication Data

Swope, Wendy.
   Wild Idaho : a guide to more than thirty recreation areas / Wendy Swope.—1st ed.
      p. cm. — (A Falcon guide)
   Includes index.
   ISBN 0–7627–2341–6
   1. Outdoor recreation—Idaho—Guidebooks. 2. Wilderness areas—Idaho—Guidebooks. 3. Idaho—Guidebooks. I. Title. II. Series.

   GV191.42.I2 S96 2002
   790'.09796—dc21

                                                                    2002069239

Manufactured in the United States of America
First Edition/First Printing

To my husband, Will, who was patient with the long nights and lost weekends that were necessary to make this book a reality. You truly are my inspiration as well as my partner.

To my children, Christina, Billy, Laura, Jenny, and Kimberly, for being my "adventure" partners. You guys are awesome.

CONTENTS

ACKNOWLEDGMENTS

When I first undertook the research of this book, I was unable to find much printed information about Idaho's wildlands. There are more than four million acres of wildlands in this state, both designated and de facto, each under their own administration. Consequently, the materials gathered for this book came from myriad sources. Special thanks go to Rick Price, Veronique Fullmer, Jennifer Jones (BLM), and Rick Just (Idaho Department of Parks and Recreation). Though I won't mention them by name, I also thank the people at the numerous agency offices who helped with technical support and information. Thanks also to Verl Duerden of Action Whitewater Adventures for introducing me, and countless others, to the wonders of the Frank Church–River of No Return Wilderness. It's people like you, who seek to protect the environment as you introduce new people to it, who will be the vanguard of the next millennium.

LEGEND

Interstate		Powerlines	
Paved Road		Pipeline	
Gravel Road (County or Forest)		Lava	
Unimproved Road		Mountain/Peak	9,782 ft.
Railroad		Elevation Point	9,782 ft. X
Featured Trail, Trailhead		Campground	
Other Trail		Picnic Area	
Pass or Saddle		Ranger Station	
Bridge		Gate	
Lake, River, Falls		Mine	
Intermittent Stream		Cabin or Building	
Spring		Ruin	
Wilderness or Wilderness Study Area Boundary		City or Town	Fruita
Roadless Area		Orientation	N
Continental Divide	CONTINENTAL DIVIDE		
National Park, Forest Boundary	SAWTOOTH N. F.	Map Scale	0 0.5 1 Miles
State Boundary	IDAHO UTAH		

STATEWIDE OVERVIEW MAP

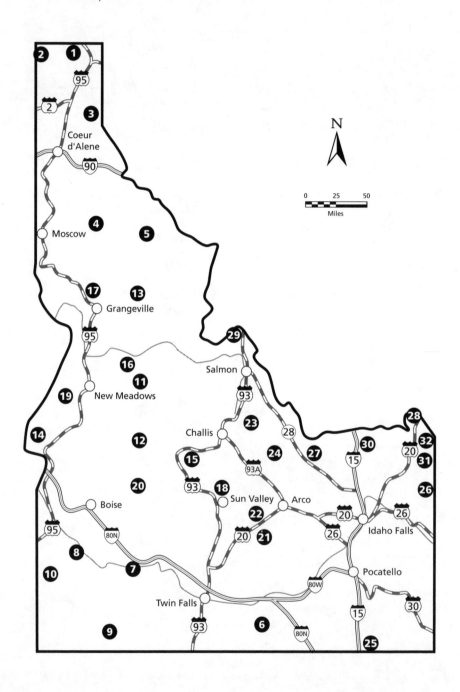

INTRODUCTION

Wilder than any other state in the lower forty-eight, Idaho is largely untracked and untrammeled. With more than four million acres of wildlands, Idaho offers unparalleled opportunity for solitude.

This book introduces you to the many diverse wild areas in the state. From vast lava fields and unmarked high-country desert to inland rain forest, Idaho helps us find and explore our natural legacy.

A visit to a "wild" area will strike an individual profoundly, whether due to the land's distinctive physical characteristics or the opportunity for solitude. We recognize wilderness when we experience it. And in order to protect it we must come to love it; in order to love it we must first know it.

This guide includes both established designated wilderness areas and lands that are essentially roadless, thus providing a wilderness experience. Some of these areas will be obvious, and some will come as a surprise until you actually explore them.

The areas that I have chosen to include in this book are in some ways subjective: these are areas—wilderness and roadless—that allow the traveler to experience "wilderness" whether an official recognition has been bestowed on it or not. Some areas were not selected even though numerous groups may be lobbying for their inclusion as wilderness. In the meantime they are heavily traveled and thus do not provide a "wild" experience. Some of the areas covered in the following pages are still under wilderness review by their respective administrative agencies, the Bureau of Land Management (BLM) or the United States Department of Agriculture–Forest Service (USDAFS). The Idaho Conservation League and other conservation groups are lobbying for specific inclusions of additional acreage.

Wildlands are classified as follows:

- **Primitive Area:** A primitive area is the Forest Service's version of a wilderness area (see definition below). This designation preserves an area's natural state by allowing no alteration or development. However, this status *does* allow for fire prevention activity.

- **Wilderness Area:** An official designation by the United States Congress that sets aside land to be preserved in its natural state. Wilderness area status prohibits all motorized activity, road-building, or commercial activity. These areas are usually defined as being undeveloped federal land of more than 5,000 acres.

- **Pioneer Area:** A roadless area that is in the process of becoming a wilderness area.

- **Wilderness Study Area:** An area under consideration by the U.S. Department of Agriculture—Forest Service (USDAFS) for possible future wilderness area designation.

- **National Reserve or Monument:** Part of the National Park classification that seeks to preserve certain sites for their natural features or historic significance.

- **National Forest Roadless Area:** This is an area that is roadless and undeveloped but not currently protected under wilderness status. A roadless area essentially offers the same type of "wild" experience as a wilderness area but is often not designated as wilderness because of economic reasons, size and location, or special-interest opposition.

- **National Wild and Scenic River:** This classification is used to distinguish and protect certain river corridors. There are three designations: wild, scenic, or recreational. Idaho is home to eight wild and scenic rivers.

- **National Recreation Area:** In 1972 Idaho's Sawtooth National Recreation Area became the first national recreation area in the state. Each recreation area is unique and managed individually; the main goal is to support recreation while preserving the singular character of the area. Depending on the recreation area, use of motorized equipment may or may not be allowed.

History of Idaho Wilderness

The history of Idaho wilderness actually starts with the many Indian tribes that made this vast and productive region home. From the Sheepeaters of the Middle Fork of the Salmon to the Kalispels of the Panhandle, evidence of their tenancy can still be found today.

In 1805 the historic Lewis and Clark expedition entered Idaho at Lemhi Valley, making the area the last of the soon-to-be fifty states to be "discovered" by whites. The expedition was seeking an overland route to the Pacific Ocean. Members of the Lemhi tribe were quite adamant that the Salmon River was not navigable. Captain Lewis, who investigated this claim as he waited for Captain Clark to join the expedition party, found the Lemhi's assessment to be quite accurate. Thus thwarted from a river passage, the expedition was forced to detour due north over Lost Trail Pass and into Montana and re-enter Idaho at Lolo Pass. They proceeded to follow the Lolo Trail, a long-used trail of the Nez Perce, through Idaho on the way to the confluence of the Clearwater, Snake, and Columbia Rivers. They then were able to travel on the Columbia River to the Pacific Ocean.

The state remained relatively undiscovered until 1843 when the Oregon Trail entered Idaho on the eastern border, near present day Montpelier, and continued to roughly follow the Snake River on its way into Oregon. Tens of thousands of immigrants traveled through Idaho each year during that great migration. Yellowstone National Park was formed in 1872, and its southwestern corner became the Idaho Territory's first protected land.

In 1873, after many broken promises by the U.S. government and shattered treaties, a segment of the Nez Perce tribe, led by Chief Joseph, refused to acknowledge a newly revised agreement. By 1877 the U.S. government ordered the tribe to leave the Wallowa Reservation and relocate to the Clearwater Reservation. The Nez Perce took flight across Idaho and into Montana, while being pursued by government soldiers. The band was attempting to seek sanctuary in Canada, but after a last desperate battle in the Bear Paw Mountains Chief Joseph was forced to surrender. The tribe was then relegated to a reservation in Oklahoma, where they remained until 1885, when they were dispersed to different reservations.

Five years later, in 1890, Idaho entered the Union as the forty-third state. Within a few years the state, as well as the federal government, began to see the value of protecting Idaho's wild spaces, and in 1924 Craters of the Moon was established as a national monument. In the 1930s Senator William Borah started working with the Forest Service to designate a portion of central Idaho as a primitive area. His work continued, but there was a general lack of wilderness legislative activity until the mid-1960s, when there arose the threat of a dam being built across the Salmon River. Senators Frank Church and Len Jordan fought this and held off the power companies. As a result of this battle, Senator Church and Senator James McClure went on to promote a bill that created the Hell's Canyon National Recreation Area. Senator Church was a strong advocate for preservation and was a leader of the successful passage of the Wilderness Act of 1964.

Governor Cecil B. Andrus picked up the torch in his four terms as governor and in his position as Secretary of the Interior during the Carter administration. His strong leadership resulted in the designation of much of the wilderness areas in Idaho today. These include the Frank Church–River of No Return Wilderness Area, the Snake River Birds of Prey Area, and the Hell's Canyon Wilderness Area.

Land Ownership in Idaho (2000)

Federal Land: 63.8%
• Forest Service: 38.6%
• Bureau of Land Management: 22.4%
• Other: approximately 2.8%

State Land: 5.1%
• Endowment Land: 4.7%
• Department of Fish and Game: 0.4%
• Department of Parks and Recreation: <0.1%

Private Land: 31.6%

County Land: 0.2%

Municipal Land: 0.04%

Trail Ratings and Rapid Classifications

Trail Ratings

Trails are rated subjectively; read the trail descriptions and peruse the United States Geological Survey (USGS) maps before attempting. The trails are rated using the following designations:

• **Easy:** These trails are relatively flat and short. People with even limited athleticism will find these trails doable; these hikes are also easy to prepare for.
• **Moderate:** These trails are longer and involve steeper grades; sometimes the trail provides a relatively easy hike, but there are steep switchbacks to the summit at the end. These hikes may also involve numerous river crossings and/or an overnight stay. If this is a river trip, it will involve hazards that require intermediate skills.
• **Strenuous:** These hikes and river trips may require an extended stay in the backcountry, they may offer very steep and prolonged grades, or require specialized navigation equipment. Several hikes, including one in the Owyhee backcountry, are possible only with alternate water sources and expert navigational skills. These can be extremely rewarding expeditions but also require technical skill.

For this guide I chose trails and river trips that are representative of the wilderness area described. Mileage designations are such:

• **Round-trip:** Indicates that the trail backtracks coming back. You will follow the same trail coming back to the trailhead as you did leaving it.
• **Loop:** This trail is a loop; you will not backtrack on the same trail.
• **One-way:** This trail or river trip indicates mileage from start to finish. Either the trail can continue on from this point or, as in the case of a river trip, is only navigable in one direction.

Rapid Classifications

White-water difficulty levels are classified by the American Whitewater Association as follows:

• **Class I:** Moving water with a few riffles and small waves. Few or no obstructions.
• **Class II:** Easy rapids with waves up to 3 feet and wide, clear channels that are obvious with scouting. Some maneuvering required.
• **Class III:** Rapids with high, irregular waves often capable of swamping an open canoe. Narrow passages that often require complex maneuvering. May require scouting from shore.
• **Class IV:** Long, difficult rapids with constricted passages that often require precise maneuvering in very turbulent waters. Scouting from shore is necessary, and conditions make rescue difficult. Generally not possible for open canoes. Boaters in covered canoes and kayaks should have the ability to Eskimo roll.
• **Class V–Class VI:** Long, very violent rapids with highly congested routes for teams of experts only. Rescue conditions are very difficult and dangerous.

Tips for River Running

1. Plan ahead. Obtain detailed river maps that describe your put-in and take-out points. Arrange for a shuttle back to your vehicle.
2. Know ahead of time the types of water hazards to expect in all types of stream flows. Find out what the white-water rating is for different sections of the river at the different stream flows.
3. Know your current stream flow. Stream flows can change dramatically in a few hours or days; this will change the whitewater rating. Know what to expect. This information can be obtained from the local BLM or Forest Service office. If they don't know, they will be able to tell you how to find out.

4. Know your craft. There are streams and rivers in Idaho appropriate for everyone from the amateur canoeist to the world-class kayaker. Be honest about your skills and your command of your craft.

5. Take appropriate gear. As with any backcountry excursion, you'll need to bring a simple first aid kit. On the water, include a set of dry clothes packed in plastic.

Wilderness Tips

Wilderness cannot remain "wild" unless each one of us does our part to keep it that way. The philosophy is simple: Leave a place looking like you haven't been there. The pro-active approach is to not only leave no trace of being there, but to maintain and improve where you've been. That would include picking up all visible trash, whether it is yours or not, and destroying fire rings after use. Idaho has an active Adopt-a-Trail Program that is invaluable to maintaining the thousands of miles of trails in the state, thus ensuring that foot traffic will not endanger delicate plants and animals. I strongly encourage your active participation in this program.

1. Plan ahead. Purchase excellent maps and plan your route carefully. Tell someone your itinerary and leave word at the appropriate agency about extended and/or potentially extended trips.
2. Know the hazards and be prepared. Bring sufficient food and gear for the trip. Bring appropriate additional gear for other pursuits as planned (rock climbing or river running).
3. Idaho is home to large and far-reaching populations of grizzly bears and wolves; they are much more widespread than the official agencies acknowledge. This is confirmed by hiker sightings and landowner reports. Even if there are no grizzly bears in the area you're exploring, black bears can be a hazard. Be aware and take appropriate precautions, such as packaging and storing food in bear-proof containers.
4. Stay on the trails. We've all seen what switchbacks eventually do to hillsides: They disintegrate them (due to erosion) and destroy plant life.
5. If you packed it in, pack it out.
6. If you're stopping at an established campsite, leave it better than when you arrived. Pack out or destroy micro-trash, leave wood for the next fire.
7. If you are making a new campsite, destroy evidence of the fire ring and all other evidence of your stay upon leaving.
8. Idaho's wilderness is so big that much of the pre-history here can be found intact. Please leave it that way. Evidence of cave paintings or even detritus

from early settlers is exciting to find and should be left as is for the next explorer.

9. *Giardia lamblia* is an intestinal parasite that can cause diarrhea, abdominal cramps, bloating, fatigue, and weight loss when ingested. Though the wilderness areas you travel look pristine and untouched, *Giardia* can be found in any water source. Treat all drinking water by boiling or using filters, chlorine, or iodine in the proper dosage.

How to Enjoy Wilderness

There are as many reasons to get out and experience Idaho's backcountry as there are people in this world. Here are a few suggestions that can enhance that enjoyment.

1. **Scenery.** As stated previously, you would be hard pressed to find such diverse terrain in any other state. Idaho contains rain forest and desert, vast lava fields, and white-water rivers. Finding a feature that leaves you awestruck is not uncommon.

2. **Wildlife.** Woodland caribou and white sturgeon as well as grizzly bear can be found on these trips. Moose, elk, and deer are thriving, as well as numerous species of birds and waterfowl. The best part is finding the animals where you don't expect them to be.

3. **Treasure hunting.** By this we mean natural treasures, like mushrooms and huckleberries. Morel mushrooms are the most sought-for fungus, and virtually all residents make some effort every spring to find these hidden gems. Morels are delicious mushrooms found in the early spring before the forest grasses start growing. Typically found growing up from under a bed of fallen leaves, this fungus has a wrinkled, dark, brown, "brain-like" cap on a narrow, beige stalk. Consult a good field guide to ensure proper identification; many forest mushrooms are extremely toxic. Morel mushrooms are also valuable commercially, and the Forest Service issues permits if you are collecting for this purpose.

    Another common but immensely popular treasure of the woods is the huckleberry. The huckleberry bush produces blue-black fruit in the fall that has a flavor described as being between a raspberry and a blueberry. The fruit is made into jam, jelly, and syrup. Most often found on sunny, south-facing slopes, the huckleberry is a favorite of bears as well as people. As with mushroom hunting, consult a good field guide for proper identification before picking and eating. Permits are required if you're harvesting huckleberries for commercial use.

4. History. Due to the remoteness of much of this land, evidence of previous inhabitants—Indian petroglyphs, stone settler's cabins, and abandoned mines—may be found intact. Please enjoy the history lessons, but leave such artifacts as you found them. Besides ensuring that future visitors will enjoy the artifacts, some of these features may be inherently unsafe (such as the mines in the Lemhi Mountains).

How to Use This Book

Think of this book as a broad-scale, textual map to be used for initial trip-planning overview, only with more information. You can sit back and decide where to go this weekend or plan a longer trip to a part of the state you've been curious about. Start with the statewide overview map to assess the geographic setting, select an area, and then read the chapter on the specific location for greater detail.

This book divides the state of Idaho into five regions: Panhandle (north), Canyonlands (southwest), North-Central, South-Central, and Eastern. Because of the vast amount of wildlands in Idaho, boundaries between the regions are imprecise. But each wildland falls logically into one of the regions based on its topography, plant communities, geographic location, or geological distinctiveness.

Each of the Idaho wildlands in this book is a contiguous, roadless expanse of undeveloped (mostly federal) land. A given wildland is managed by one or more of four federal agencies: the National Park Service; Fish and Wildlife Service; Bureau of Land Management; and the Forest Service. Portions of some of the areas also contain State of Idaho, individual, and corporate land. In terms of number of areas and acreage controlled, the Forest Service is by far the major operator.

Trip planning information for each wildland is presented as follows:

The Maps—The statewide overview map on page x shows the thirty-two areas covered in the book. A more detailed map accompanies the information block for each wildland, distinguishing between wilderness and nonwilderness, showing major trails and access points, and indicating the driving distance from featured trailheads to the nearest highway or town. These maps are an important reference for trip planning, but they are no substitute for the applicable topographic and travel plan maps listed in each information block.

Information Blocks—These "at-a-glance" sections contain quick facts, including:

1. *Location*—the direction and straight-line distance to the wildland from the largest and/or nearest town.

2. *Size*—measured as the total contiguous roadless area in acres, regardless of ownership or land status, based upon the best available information.

3. *Administration*—names the federal or state agencies and offices responsible for management.

4. *Management status*—reveals the area's designation as Wilderness, Wilderness Study Area, National Forest Roadless Area, etc. Since status changes continually, this category gives *some* idea as to whether a portion of a Roadless Area is slated for future resource development. A list of agencies and groups involved in wilderness studies and protection is presented in Appendix B.

5. *Ecosystems*—based largely on the broad Kuchler classifications used by the Forest Service for ecosystem management.

6. *Elevation range*—minimum and maximum elevations at obvious landmarks.

7. *System trails*—estimated distances of designated or numbered trails that may or may not be regularly maintained.

8. *Maximum core to perimeter distance*—the longest straight-line mileage from inside the wilderness area to the closest road. There are exceptions, but this mileage gives you a general idea of the wildness of the country in terms of remoteness and solitude.

9. *Activities*—those nonmotorized pursuits for which the area is best suited, both from a legal standpoint (in the case of wilderness) and the physical lay of the land. Hiking is common to all the areas.

10. *Best months*—what are considered to be the best months to travel and explore these areas.

11. *Maps*—a listing of the applicable agency travel or management plan map, which is usually small scale (0.5 inch/mile planimetric); the applicable wilderness map on a contour base; and all the 1:1,000,000 scale USGS topographic maps that cover the wildland, starting at the northwest corner. Topographic maps are listed for each area in Appendix D.

12. *Overview*—captures a bit of the "personality" of the country, including flora and fauna, geology, historical significance, and major points of interest.

13. *Recreational uses*—expands on suitable activities, with occasional trip ideas presented as well. In keeping with the idea of balancing land use, the more heavily visited trails and sites are indicated, where applicable. Your route may still include these locations, but at least you'll know ahead of time that your chances for solitude are reduced.

14. *How to get there*—contains detailed driving instructions to the trailheads or jumping-off points for the sample trips. Road designations are abbreviated—after first use—as follows: FR=Forest Road; I=Interstate; ID=Idaho highway; US=U.S. highway.

15. *Sample trip ideas*—one or more trips—mostly lightly used locations to help redistribute use—are suggested for each wildland. These suggestions cover a variety of activities, travel modes, and seasons. Most of the sample trips are on established trails to lessen the impact on pristine areas. Those who plan to travel through trackless terrain must know how to use a compass and a topo map and do everything possible to travel lightly in a fragile environment. And while rating hikes as "easy," "moderate," or "strenuous" is subjective, some generalities apply: For example, a short hike on a level trail would be easy for most people, while a long hike through heavy brush and cliff terrain would be strenuous for virtually anyone.

North: Panhandle

Long Canyon/Selkirk Crest

Location: Northern Idaho, 26 miles northwest of Bonners Ferry.
Size: Selkirk Crest 32,677 acres (USDAFS); Long Canyon 26,497 acres (roadless).
Administration: USDAFS, Kanisku National Forest.
Management status: Roadless, proposed wilderness.
Ecosystems: Pacific rain forest/alpine meadow province characterized by glaciated mountains with moraines; Precambrian metasedimentary rock; Douglas fir forest type; numerous streams.
Elevation range: 3,000 feet within Long Canyon to 7,670 feet at Parker Peak.
System trails: 37 miles.
Maximum core to perimeter distance: 9 miles.
Activities: Hiking, fishing, and mushroom hunting.
Best months: June, July, August, and September.
Maps: Shorty Peak-ID; Smith Falls-ID; Smith Peaks-ID; Pyramid Peak-ID; The Wigwams-ID; Roman Nose-ID; Mount Roothaan-ID; Dodge Peak-ID (USGS 1:1,000,000); Kanisku Forest Service Map.

OVERVIEW The Selkirk Mountains lie 300 miles inland from the Pacific Ocean and extend 250 miles, roughly south to north, from Idaho to British Columbia. The Selkirk Crest lies at the southernmost Idaho point of the Selkirk Mountains and continues along a narrow ridge scattered with twenty-four alpine lakes. Long Canyon extends northeast from the crest and is filled with intermediate and old growth forests of western red cedar, western hemlock, western larch, Douglas fir, grand fir, and western white pine. Spruce fir forest is seen at the higher elevations of this 18-mile-long canyon.

The entire mountain range receives a lot of precipitation year-round—abundant rain in the summer months and heavy, deep snow in the winter—contributing to the growth of huge western cedars, Douglas fir, and spruce covered with moss and lichen. Other common trees include Engelmann spruce, mountain hemlock, pacific yew, western red cedar, and black cottonwood.

Many large animal species make their homes in the dense forests, including grizzly and black bear, moose, and white-tailed deer. The numerous lakes and streams are filled with rainbow and brook trout and also attract a wide variety of waterfowl.

Estimated to have evolved approximately 400 million years ago, the

IA   LONG CANYON/SELKIRK CREST

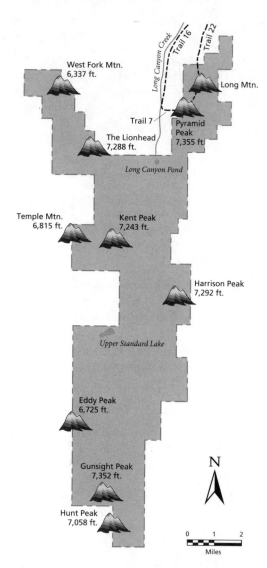

endangered Kootenai River sturgeon is a living "dinosaur." The Kootenai River sturgeon is a subgroup of white sturgeon, the largest freshwater fish in North America and capable of attaining weights of 1,500 pounds and lengths of more than 20 feet. The Kootenai white sturgeon population is landlocked and contained within 168 miles of the river and is therefore incapable of attaining these great sizes. The largest reported sturgeon caught in the Kootenai weighed in at 350 pounds (1995). White sturgeon are long lived; they reach maturity

1B LONG CANYON/SELKIRK CREST (LONG CANYON TRAIL)

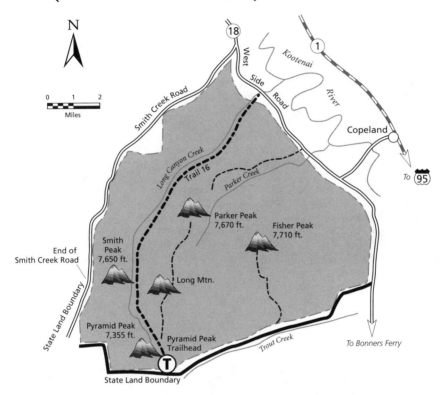

at approximately twenty years old and can live to well over eighty. The delayed onset of maturity (and thus ability to spawn) and changes in habitat (such as logging operations and farming practices in the area, which can affect water quality) have adversely affected the sturgeon's spawning habits and the survival rate of fry. The Kootenai River sturgeon is currently listed as a Species of Special Concern, and the harvesting of them is prohibited.

The Long Canyon/Selkirk Crest area (along with the Salmo–Priest proposed wilderness area) is also unique in that it is home to woodland caribou, the only such herd in the lower forty-eight states. At present fewer than one hundred woodland caribou live in the Selkirk Mountains of northern Idaho and northeastern Washington. Caribou are especially suited to the conditions found in the Selkirks; their hollow hair provides insulation against the cold and their wide hooves provide traction and support in deep snow. Woodland caribou subsist on a diet of moss and lichen, found growing abundantly on the trees in this damp climate. These animals are very territorial and make their year-round

Long Canyon Creek flows into the Kootenai River.

home within a small range; they do not migrate to lower elevations in the winter months. The woodland caribou is listed as endangered under the Endangered Species Act.

Both the Kootenai white sturgeon and the woodland caribou have the support of federal and state agencies as well as regional conservation groups. Their common goal is to revive these species as well as to restore and/or maintain their habitats.

RECREATIONAL USES This area is largely unprotected, but its dearth of trails and the remoteness of its location have helped keep it in a pristine state. In particular, Long Canyon's steep and narrow formation has served to protect it from logging companies who are unable to extract its resources profitably.

Since most of this area is extremely wet, mushroom hunting is a very popular, and profitable, pastime; so much so that the Forest Service issues permits and limits on how many pounds can be harvested.

The abundance of lakes and streams provides ample opportunities for canoeing, kayaking, and fishing. The big, deep lakes in the region are home to Kamloops trout and Kokanee and Chinook salmon. The area's smaller and shallower waters provide excellent habitat for numerous species of trout, including rainbow, cutthroat, brook, and German brown. Warm-water species such as bass and perch can also be found.

Hiking the backcountry is fairly easy as the terrain does not require huge elevation gains. The opportunity to experience this unique biology is a big draw; however, the wet conditions in this rain forest climate can be discouraging, and little-used trails can quickly become overgrown with brush.

HOW TO GET THERE *Long Canyon Trail:* From Bonners Ferry drive 15 miles north on U.S. Highway 95 until Idaho Highway 1 bears off to the left. Keep left on ID 1 and proceed until you find the Copeland turnoff. Turn west and drive 10 miles, crossing over the Kootenai River, then head north on County Road 18 (West Side Road) for 6.5 miles. The trailhead is well marked as Canyon Creek Trail at the gravel pits. It is on the left side of the road about 0.5 mile after crossing over the Canyon Creek bridge.

Extended Hike

Long Canyon Trail

Distance: 18 miles one way.
Difficulty: Moderately strenuous.
Topo maps: Smith Peak-ID; Pyramid Peak-ID; Shorty Peak-ID; Smith Falls-ID.

Few spots in the state of Idaho can offer hikers a trip through an actual rain forest, but this trail does. The canyon provides an opportunity to investigate the various species of moss and lichen covering gigantic trees, as well as a chance to view grizzly bears. Mushroom hunting is a popular activity in September and many varieties, including the delicious morels, can be found.

The hike is long but not particularly difficult as it follows Long Canyon Creek upriver from its ultimate destination into the Kootenai River. The hike can be further extended by taking side trips to nearby lakes.

The canyon is 2.5 miles wide on average with a vertical gain of 2,000–3,000 feet from the canyon floor to the ridges. The trail (Long Canyon Trail #16) starts at the Canyon Creek trailhead and travels down into the narrowest part of the canyon, through pine and aspen forest. The trail heads upstream of Long Canyon Creek and enters the rain forest approximately 8 miles into the hike. Twelve miles into the hike the route will leave the creek and head left (east) for a short, steep climb past Pyramid Peak and to Pyramid Pass. From this point it accesses Trail #7 and the Pyramid Lake trailhead. At the trailhead Forest Road #634 takes you 10 miles back to County Road 18 (West Side Road).

Salmo–Priest

2

Location: Extreme northwest corner of Idaho, 38 miles north of Nordman.
Size: 14,700 acres.
Administration: USDAFS, Kanisku National Forest.
Management status: Proposed wilderness.
Ecosystems: Pacific rain forest/alpine meadow province characterized by glaciated mountains with moraines; Precambrian metasedimentary rock; Douglas fir forest type; numerous streams.
Elevation range: 2,720 feet on the Upper Priest River to 7,572 feet at Snowy Top Peak.
System trails: 22 miles.
Maximum core to perimeter distance: 12 miles.
Activities: Hiking and fishing.
Best months: June, July, and August.
Maps: Continental Mountain-ID; Grass Mountain-ID; Upper Priest Lake-ID; Caribou Creek-ID; Priest Lake NW-ID (USGS 1:1,000,000).

OVERVIEW The Salmo–Priest proposed wilderness area is part of the Selkirk Mountain range and is a great example of an inland rain forest. The area is located in the extreme northwest corner of Idaho and is geographically part of the larger 41,335-acre Salmo–Priest Wilderness in Washington. This landscape continues on into British Columbia to the north.

The Salmo–Priest area is bordered on the southeast by Upper Priest Lake, which is connected to the main Priest Lake by the 2.5-mile-long Priest River. The area received its name from the Blackrobes, or Jesuit missionary priests, who first visited this area in the 1840s and established schools to serve the local Indian tribes. "Salmo" is the genus for trout as well as salmon.

An Upper Priest Lake scenic area was established in 1986 and lies due west of Upper Priest Lake. Its purpose is to preserve the natural wilderness and recreational values along the shores of Upper Priest Lake.

Water is the predominant feature here, influencing every aspect of the area. Abundant precipitation and warm temperatures encourage the growth of the magnificent, 3,000-year-old red cedars found here. Douglas fir, Engelmann spruce, mountain hemlock, Pacific yew, and black cottonwood are common and often found generously covered with moss and lichen. Snow accumulates to depths of more than 15 feet at higher elevations; the lower valleys are blessed with equally abundant rainfall. Birds find the plentiful moisture attractive, and

2 SALMO–PRIEST

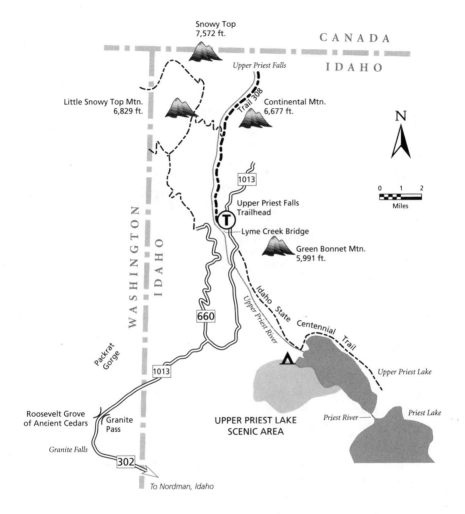

many species are plentiful, including geese, ducks, osprey, bald eagles, wood-peckers, owls, grouse, and bluebirds.

The Salmo–Priest is also home to many large and endangered animal species, including grizzly and black bear, gray wolf, bighorn sheep, elk, lynx, and bobcat. The Salmo–Priest also supports the woodland caribou that live within the Selkirk Mountains. (See the Long Canyon/Selkirk Crest chapter for more information on the woodland caribou.)

Priest Lake is the prelude to Upper Priest Lake and the Salmo–Priest area.

RECREATIONAL USES This area has yet to gain protected status, but it sees very little use outside of fall hunters. Its remote location is a plus: Visitors cannot simply drive by and stop here—they have to make a concerted effort to reach the Salmo–Priest. Roads into the Salmo–Priest dead-end, and the nearest towns offer little attraction in and of themselves. The main attractions here are solitude and the opportunity to view a section of Idaho that is truly unique.

The plant and animal life is reminiscent of rain forests and, as such, it is completely different from any other area of the state. Similar to treasure hunting but much more rewarding, huckleberry hunting and mushroom picking are ways to enjoy the area. The forest floor sports unique flora such as carpet mosses, Canadian dogwood, maidenhair fern, and calypso orchids. In fact researchers believe that some regional flora may have potential medicinal uses.

The Upper Priest River, listed as one of America's Wild and Scenic rivers under the National Wild and Scenic Rivers Act, is good for kayaking. The white water here runs up to Class IV during the spring runoff.

HOW TO GET THERE From Priest River take Idaho Highway 57 north for 38 miles to Nordman. Here you access Granite Creek Road (Forest Road 302) heading northwest out of Nordman. The road follows Granite Creek, goes over Granite Pass, and down to Forest Road 1013 to the trailhead located just past the Lime Creek Bridge. (Note that 12 miles north of Nordman and in Washington are Granite Falls and the Roosevelt Grove of Ancient Cedars. The sights here are unique, and there is an interpretive center.) From here the road continues through Packrat Gorge and then over Granite Pass and back into Idaho. From Granite Pass drive 9.5 miles to the trailhead for Upper Priest Falls.

Day Hike

Upper Priest Falls/ Idaho State Centennial Trail (Trail #308)

Distance: 16 miles round-trip.
Difficulty: Easy.
Topo maps: Continental Mountain-ID; Upper Priest Lake-ID.

This hike follows the Idaho State Centennial Trail, missing the Canadian border by 0.5 mile. This trip is suggested for mid-summer when road conditions are optimum (dry).

The hike is on a straight and easy trail that follows and crosses over the Upper Priest River. For this reason, and the ever-present promise of rainfall, waterproof clothing is recommended. Mushroom hunting is a good pastime here; however, due to diverse varieties, a good field guide is advisable. Wildlife viewing should be easy, with numerous species abundant on the hike, particularly squirrels, deer, and birdlife. The opportunity to view woodland caribou should not be discounted.

A short side trail of 6 miles round trip can be made to Little Snowy Top Mountain. This trail has more than ninety switchbacks but gains only 400 feet in elevation. After the easy initial hike it's worth the added effort for this view of the surrounding terrain.

Scotchman Peaks

3

Location: Northern Idaho, 25 miles southeast of Sandpoint.
Size: 23,900 acres (in Idaho).
Administration: USDAFS, Kootenai and Idaho Panhandle National Forests.
Management status: Roadless, proposed wilderness.
Ecosystems: Northern Rocky Mountain coniferous forest/alpine meadow province characterized by glaciated mountains with moraines; Precambrian metasedimentary rock; Douglas fir and western ponderosa pine forest types; old growth cedar-hemlock forests in low-elevation valleys; numerous streams.
Elevation range: 3,837 feet at Lake Pend Oreille to 7,009 feet at Scotchman Peak.
System trails: 30 miles.
Maximum core to perimeter distance: 24 miles.
Activities: Hiking, fishing, horseback riding, and cross-country skiing.
Best months: June, July, and August. February for skiing.
Maps: Trestle Peak-ID; Benning Mountain-ID/MT; Clark Fork-ID; Scotchman Peak-ID/MT (USGS 1:1,000,000).

OVERVIEW This roadless area is commonly called Scotchman Peaks, though it actually takes its name from the one peak—Scotchman Peak, so named for its resemblance to a Scotchman in native attire. The area surrounding the Scotchman Peaks was created thousands of years ago when Lake Pend Oreille was part of a massive inland sea called Lake Missoula. The lake was created by glaciers, brought down from the Purcell Trench that extends from Canada through the Kootenai Valley, carving a path through the area. The Selkirk Mountains now rise to the north, the Coeur d'Alene Mountains rise to the south, and the Cabinet Mountains (and Scotchman Peak) rise to the east.

Scotchman Peak climbs to a height of 7,009 feet, towering 5,000 feet above the east side of Lake Pend Oreille. Northern Idaho is known for its dense forests, not its high peaks, so Scotchman's mountaintop view of two states and Canada is impressive for the area. Scotchman Peak is relatively treeless. Boulder fields interspersed with vast meadows are the main feature, and cedar, hemlock, and white pine are predominant in the forested areas. The entire area—Idaho and Montana—has been proposed for wilderness designation, and although Scotchman Peak itself is in Idaho, most of the roadless acres recommended for wilderness by conservation groups lie over the border in Montana.

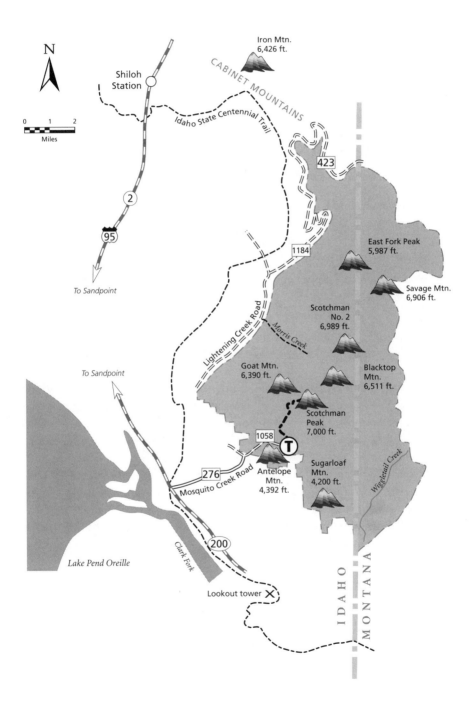

Scotchman Peak rises above Lake Pend Oreille, one of Idaho's largest glacial lakes. At 94,600 acres and 43 miles long, this lake is one of the largest in North America. Lake Pend Oreille supposedly got its name from the French *pende-loque oreille* (earring), referring to the earrings worn by a local Native American tribe, the Kalispel. The lake boasts a depth of more than 1,225 feet. The United States Navy created the Farragut Naval Training Station on the shores of Lake Pend Oreille in World War II. During the war, more than 300,000 enlisted men passed through this station, located at the southwestern tip of the lake. The Navy maintains a presence in the town of Bayview, where it continues to design and test submarines.

The lake also supports an important fishery, with record numbers of brown, rainbow, and cutthroat trout; bull trout (landlocked Dolly Varden); kokanee salmon; largemouth bass; crappie; and mackinaw residing within. Other species of fish include pumpkin-seed sunfish, perch, peno, squawfish, tench, and sculpin.

Wildlife is plentiful on and around Scotchman Peak, with mountain goats being the most interesting residents. Eagles, grizzly bears, gray wolves, elk, fishers, pine martens, wolverines, and boreal owls also reside here and into the roadless areas stretching east from the peak into Montana.

RECREATIONAL USES This area is spectacular for its view of Lake Pend Oreille and the opportunity for real backcountry solitude.

Hiking, horseback riding, and hunting are popular here, and abundant snow coupled with big meadows make it a good place to go cross-country skiing. Hikes need not be limited to Scotchman Peak itself but can be easily extended into Montana for extended backcountry experiences, though few good trails exist. Forest roads are few, although there is a dense cluster of them in the vicinity of the Moose Mountains that attracts a lot of over-the-road attention. Two branches of the Idaho State Centennial Trail are good trails through the backcountry area into Montana. The northern branch travels from the town of Clark Fork due north along the spine of the Cabinet Mountains 31 miles to Iron Mountain, where the trail turns sharply to the west 10 miles to the Shiloh Station along Idaho Highway 95 (Idaho Highway 2). See the Falcon Guide *Wild Montana* by Bill Cunningham for a description of the Scotchman Peaks roadless area in Montana.

HOW TO GET THERE *Scotchman Peak:* From Sandpoint drive 23 miles east on Idaho Highway 200 to Clark Fork. Turn left onto Mosquito Creek Road (Forest Road 276) and travel 2 miles to Forest Road 1058. Turn left onto this road and follow it to the end. Many logging trails branch off from these roads, so pay attention to your maps.

The Scotchman Peak area overlooks magnificent Lake Pend Oreille.

Day Hike or Cross-country Ski Trip

Scotchman Peak

Distance: 8 miles round-trip.
Difficulty: Moderately strenuous.
Topo map: Scotchman Peak-ID/MT.

The trail is not a difficult one, but it does make a steady gain in elevation to the summit, approximately 4,000 feet. If you are traveling on skis, the first half of the trail (approximately 2 miles) will suffice for a full day. There are plenty of open meadows and a gentle grade interspersed with stands of cedar, hemlock, and white fir. There are fantastic views of Lake Pend Oreille to the west.

The last half of the trail switchbacks and climbs at a higher grade toward the summit. Here the trail is more densely forested, so it is more conducive to hiking than skiing.

Northern Idaho's history is studded with forest fires; evidence of these can be seen from Scotchman Peak. An abandoned Forest Service lookout tower is located at the summit. The tower is no longer maintained and is in poor condition and should not be explored.

Mallard–Larkins Pioneer Area

4

Location: Northern Idaho, 60 miles east of Moscow.
Size: 20,000 acres; another 150,000 acres is proposed for wilderness designation.
Administration: USDAFS, Clearwater and Idaho Panhandle National Forests.
Management status: Roadless, proposed wilderness.
Ecosystems: Northern Rocky Mountain coniferous forest/alpine meadow province characterized by glaciated mountains, granitic in the south, with argillite pinnacles on ridges to the north; Douglas fir and western ponderosa pine forest types containing ponderosa pine at lower, drier elevations, along with cedar, larch, and hemlock in stream bottoms, and subalpine tundra along open slopes and high ridges; abundant perennial streams, wet meadows, and mountain lakes at higher elevations.
Elevation range: 3,920 feet at the St. Joe River to 7,043 feet at East Sister Peak.
System trails: 54 miles.
Maximum core to perimeter distance: 18 miles.
Activities: Hiking, camping, fishing, and hunting.
Best months: June, July, and August.
Maps: Montana Peak-ID; Bathtub Mountain-ID; Buzzard Roost-ID; Mallard Peak-ID (USGS 1:1,000,000).

OVERVIEW The name of this area comes from two prominent peaks, Mallard (6,870 feet) and Larkins (6,661 feet). The proposed wilderness area includes Five Lakes Butte on the east and Foehl Creek on the west. The north side of the Mallard–Larkins Pioneer Area drains into the St. Joe River and forms the largest remaining unroaded section of the Idaho Panhandle National Forest. This roadless area encompasses the rugged mountains between the St. Joe and Clearwater Rivers. South of the Clearwater River there are a substantial number of logging and Forest Service roads.

The Mallard–Larkins Pioneer Area is comprised of steep mountains and sharp ridges, interspersed with thirty-eight subalpine lakes mainly clustered around Larkins Peak. The main creeks in the Pioneer Area, Foehl, Canyon, and Sawtooth, drain south into the Clearwater River. The creeks in the northern portion of the Mallard–Larkins, the Bluff, Mosquito, Fly, and Beaver Creeks, flow north into the St. Joe River.

Northern Idaho's forests, seemingly abundant and limitless, make the area especially attractive to lumber interests. Unfortunately for the Mallard–Larkins, not only is the timber plentiful, but the terrain does not prohibit

4   MALLARD–LARKINS PIONEER AREA

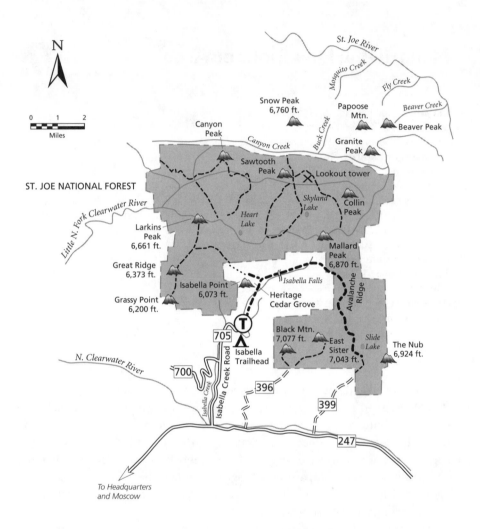

access. Conservationists have worked toward wilderness designation for this area; to date the Forest Service has granted it "Pioneer Area" status.

The Mallard–Larkins Pioneer Area is the largest unroaded elk habitat in the St. Joe drainage. The thriving elk populations use the Mallard–Larkins as a migration route as well as for critical winter range. Safe access to migratory routes enables these animals to travel to winter ranges where food and shelter are adequate. Because of the difficulty that hunters have accessing the area (few roads), a high percentage of mature bulls live in this area, making for a very stable population. The mountain goat population is thriving, and deer, moose, black bear, and cougar also inhabit this rugged area.

RECREATIONAL USES The area is popular for hiking, fishing, and viewing and hunting wildlife. Several old fire lookout stations are still standing, and some are available for overnight rental. A lookout station at the summit of Sawtooth Peak provides a great view of small lakes to the south, the drainage of Sawtooth Creek and surrounding peaks, including Collins, Canyon, Snow, Papoose, and Granite. Most lookout stations provide access to good trails; check with the Forest Service office for maps and availability.

There are four species of trout, as well as bass, Kokanee salmon, and steelhead in the high mountain lakes. Hunting, however, is the big draw. In fall the large population of elk, with many mature bulls, makes the effort of long hikes worthwhile to many hunters. Bear, mountain goat, mule and white-tailed deer, and mountain lion are also plentiful in the area.

Hiking provides opportunity for solitude; the surrounding mountains are not wilderness areas, but they are essentially roadless and so densely forested that travel off the generally good trails is difficult at best. The land bordering the Mallard–Larkins to the east and stretching to Lolo Pass is particularly tough. If you can overcome these barriers, though, you'll be treated to breathtaking scenery, solitude, and the chance to see mountain goats. Due to the added trail traffic that hunting season brings, hike at alternate times. Check local game regulations to avoid conflicts.

HOW TO GET THERE *Isabella Creek:* From Kamiah take U.S. Highway 12 north for 15 miles to the turnoff for Idaho Highway 11 east. Travel this road 33 miles to Headquarters. From Headquarters drive 19 miles to Isabella Creek Road (Forest Road 705). The trailhead lies just over 1 mile up this road.

Day Hike

Isabella Creek to the Nub

Distance: 12 miles round-trip.
Difficulty: Easy to moderate.
Topo maps: Mallard Peak-ID.

This trail starts from Isabella Creek trailhead at the Isabella Creek Campground and follows the canyon for 2 miles. Take the trail to the left for a side trip to the Heritage Cedar Grove, approximately 2 miles round-trip. These trees are estimated to be hundreds of years old.

Once back on the original trail, head east. The trail will follow Isabella Creek for 2 miles until its arrival at Isabella Falls; then make a short climb to the ridgeline. The trail intersects with another here; you take the right-hand (south) path. Two miles farther along the ridgeline the trail crosses Avalanche Ridge.

There is a fire lookout tower visible approximately 2 miles on the right. This tower, as with most fire lookout towers, is available for overnight camping; many good trails intersect with them. Check with the Forest Service for availability.

From Avalanche Ridge the trail will start a descent toward Forest Road 247. Fine fishing can be found at Slide Lake, and a moderately difficult side trip to the top of the Nub is an option, too.

Great Burn

Location: Northern Idaho and northwest Montana, 50 miles west of Missoula, Montana.
Size: 106,033 acres.
Administration: USDAFS, Lolo and Clearwater National Forests.
Management status: Roadless, proposed wilderness.
Ecosystems: Northern Rocky Mountain coniferous forest/alpine meadow province characterized by glaciated mountains, granitic in the south, with argillite pinnacles on ridges to the north; Douglas fir and western ponderosa pine forest types containing ponderosa pine at lower, drier elevations, along with cedar, larch, and hemlock in stream bottoms (large areas of spruce-fir occur with some lodgepole pine in burns), and subalpine tundra along open slopes and high ridges; abundant perennial streams, wet meadows, and mountain lakes at higher elevations.
Elevation range: 3,200 feet at Cayuse Creek to 7,930 feet at Rhodes Peak.
System trails: 288 miles.
Maximum core to perimeter distance: 18 miles.
Activities: Hiking, backpacking, horseback riding, cross-country skiing, and fishing.
Best months: June, July, and August.
Maps: Hoodoo Pass-ID/MT; Straight Peak-ID/MT; Bruin Hill-ID/MT; Schley Mtn.-ID/MT; Rhodes Peak-ID/MT; Granite Pass-ID/MT (USGS 1:1,000,000); 1994 Lolo National Forest Visitor Map.

OVERVIEW The Great Burn got its name and distinctive open country from the famous fire of 1910. The fire was the result of several seasons of drought conditions that made for tinder-dry forests. During the summer of 1910, numerous fires sprang up in Idaho and Montana. The coup de grace arrived in August when the winds picked up. The winds drove the existing fires to ever greater heights and consolidated the burning acreage. By the time the conflagration was contained, 4,700 square miles of Lolo and Clearwater National Forest, more than three million acres in Idaho and Montana, and one-third of the town of Wallace, Idaho, were destroyed. Along with an untold number of citizens, fifty-seven firefighters lost their lives in the fires, most of the bodies recovered from the St. Joe drainage. As a result of the devastation, the Weeks Law was passed in 1911. This law provided for federal and state cooperation in the case of interstate wildfires.

The fire destroyed most of the old-growth cedar and hemlock and left in its wake ground covered largely with low-growing brush. The trees have not regrown in the area, and so it has regained little of its original commercial value.

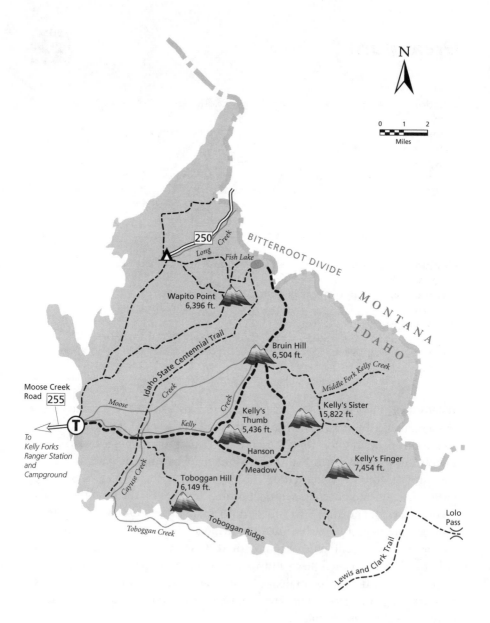

Thus, the fire contributed to the fact that the Great Burn continues to be a roadless area today.

The Great Burn lies on both sides of the Bitterroot Divide; several important river drainages are contained within it. Kelly, Cayuse, and Toboggan Creeks serve as critical trout fisheries, and Kelly and Cayuse Creeks provide secluded spawning grounds for Chinook salmon and steelhead.

The Great Burn also provides lush habitat for one of the largest elk herds in the country. The area's isolation has encouraged the growth and development of the largest number of trophy bull elk in Idaho. The Great Burn is so extensive and so protected that these herds do not migrate. Other species are abundant, including black bear, moose, deer, pine marten, mountain goat, cougar, and a few wolves. The wildlife has been rich and varied for a long time, as evidenced by the fact that the Nez Perce have traditionally hunted here as well as traveled to the productive buffalo hunting grounds in Montana using what is known today as the Lolo National Historic Trail. The trail forms the southern border of the Great Burn. Lolo Pass was the route taken by Lewis and Clark in 1805 as they searched for a passage to the Pacific Ocean. They undertook this expedition after they had tried, and failed, to find a way to ford the Salmon River farther south. (See chapter 24 for more information.)

The Nez Perce considered this portion of Idaho their ancestral homeland. Sadly, many were eventually forced onto a reservation in Oklahoma; the rest were sent to the Coleville Reservation in Washington State. In 1877 Chief Joseph resisted the American government's efforts to force the tribe onto reservations. After months of fighting, evasion, and appeals to the federal government, he was forced to acquiesce.

RECREATIONAL USES With the irresistible draw of the huge trophy elk population, hunting is the prime recreational activity here in the Great Burn. Hunters from around the state put in their applications early for the opportunity to hunt this area. Since this land is essentially roadless, most of the hunting is done on foot and on horseback. If you wish to experience backcountry solitude, skip visiting during hunting season. Not only are there more people in the woods in the fall, but the trailheads and campsites become congested with hunters and their gear. Check with Idaho Fish and Game for current hunting-season dates.

Fishing is also a great recreational pursuit in the Great Burn and is not dependent on a short season, like hunting. Fishermen have the entire summer season to enjoy their sport and so do not substantially contribute to trail congestion. The rare westslope cutthroat and golden trout as well as the more common species of trout swim in the high lakes and streams. Most of the trails in the Great Burn are closed to off-road vehicle use, making the area all the more valuable for a quality, backcountry experience.

The effects of the great fires of 1910 are still very evident today, and area universities regularly conduct on-site classes at various locations.

HOW TO GET THERE From the town of Headquarters, take Forest Road 247/Idaho Highway 11 north 36 miles to the north fork of the Clearwater River. The Bungalow Ranger Station is located here. Take the left fork of Forest Road 250 east for 12 miles to the Kelly Forks Ranger Station. Head straight on Forest Road 255, also known as Moose Creek Road, for 9 miles.

Extended Hike and Overnighter

Hanson Ridge Loop Trail

Distance: 32-mile loop.
Difficulty: Moderately strenuous.
Topo map: Bruin Hill-ID.

This trail is a great extended fishing trip and includes two branches of the Idaho State Centennial Trail. The trail follows the Kelly Creek drainage; fishing for native cutthroat trout is a big draw here. Five miles up the creek another canyon forms to the left, with a tributary of Kelly Creek emptying into the main creek. The trail forks here with the right-hand branch circling Kelly's Thumb and the left following the smaller Kelly Creek drainage. If you take the left fork, you'll follow the canyon for another 3 miles. If you take the right fork, you'll climb 1 mile to the top of Hanson Ridge. Here there are excellent views of the peaks that form the border of Idaho and Montana. The trail then drops slightly in elevation before climbing a small mountain and dropping down to Fish Lake. There is superb fishing here, and this makes the perfect spot for camping, right on the Idaho/Montana border.

Due west of the lake is the west fork of the Idaho State Centennial Trail. From the lake it's a mild climb back up to the ridgeline and then back to the trailhead, taking the trail that encircled Kelly's Thumb.

Southwest: Canyonlands

City of Rocks

Location: Southern Idaho, 50 miles south of Burley, 2 miles west of Almo.
Size: 14,300 acres (one-third of which is privately owned).
Administration: NPS, City of Rocks National Reserve; Idaho Department of Parks and Recreation.
Management status: Nonwilderness.
Ecosystems: High desert bioregion characterized by high, rolling plateaus supporting sagebrush or shad scale, mixed with short grasses; mountains are comprised of exposed granitic rock, isolated stands of junipers, and sparse sagebrush; basins are narrow and characterized by outcroppings of tall, granite columns.
Elevation range: 5,800 feet on the basin floor to 8,867 feet at Graham Peak.
System trails: 20 miles.
Maximum core to perimeter distance: 1.8 miles
Activities: Rock climbing, hiking, mountain biking, walking, camping, photography, cross-country skiing, snowshoeing, and ice climbing.
Best months: March and April.
Maps: Almo-ID; Cache Peak-ID (USGS 1:1,000,000); City of Rocks Visitor's Guide.

OVERVIEW City of Rocks is not technically a roadless area; however, the wide availability of hiking opportunities and the remoteness of some of the climbing spires provide ample wilderness-type experiences. The roads within the reserve are dirt but are well-maintained throughout the summer months; they are usually closed in early winter.

From the tiny town of Almo, drive up a steep and narrow canyon before entering the City of Rocks. The view from this vantage point is startling. This narrow basin and sagebrush-coated country is studded with surreal granite columns, some reaching sixty stories tall. They appear to have been arranged in a "studiously random" fashion, as if the cousins of the architects at Stonehenge had had a hand in it.

A number of these formations are more than 2.5 billion years old, among the oldest exposed rocks in North America, and were formed primarily through erosion. The formations are composed of granitic rock (light-colored, course-grained rock with salt and pepper specks) formed deep within the earth's surface.

During this country's great westward migration, the City of Rocks area was an important landmark and stage stop along the California Trail and the Salt

6   CITY OF ROCKS

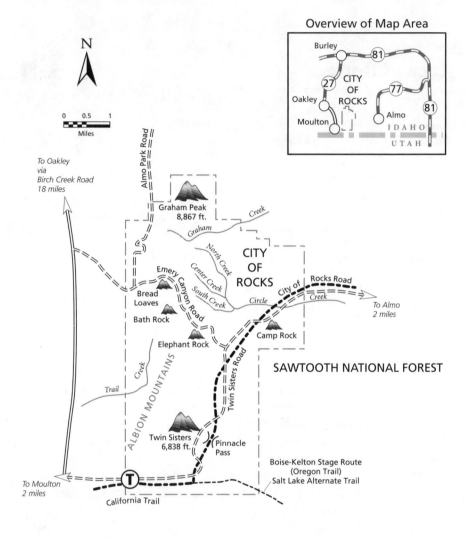

Overview of Map Area

Lake Alternate Trail, beginning in 1843. An estimated 50,000 people traveled these trails through the City of Rocks in 1852, the time of peak migration, as they made their way to the California gold fields. The stage route from Kelton, Utah, to Boise, Idaho, passed through here from 1869 to 1883. Many pioneers wrote their names in axle grease on the rocks adjacent to the trail, some of which are still visible today. They are not marked, but the markings can be readily seen under protective rock overhangs and in shallow caves.

The colorful little town of Oakley is an access point to City of Rocks. The uniquely colored, flat stone that is mined here has been used throughout the country.

The rock formations that were used as landmarks by early pioneers provide a variety of rock climbing opportunities today. About 600 routes have been described to date; the 100–300–foot spires provide most of the climbing opportunities. The smaller, rounded formations provide easy and convenient climbs for even the least athletic. For more information on these climbs, see *City of Rocks, Idaho: A Climber's Guide* by Dave Bingham (Globe Pequot Press/ Chockstone).

These rock formations provide habitat for many wildlife species. Rarely seen but constituting a viable population in the reserve is the cougar. This animal hunts nocturnally but occasionally its tracks can be seen leading to and from dens. The cougar's main prey, white-tailed and mule deer, is commonly seen as you explore this reserve.

City of Rocks is considered to be high desert, and the predominant plant life is sagebrush and native grasses, with juniper supported at higher elevations. The area does have several intermittent streams that flow in early spring.

RECREATIONAL USES The City of Rocks is not a roadless area, but the nature of the activity it draws tends to preserve its "wild" character. The reserve draws a considerable number of climbers of all abilities, and this generates the most visitors. Since the primitive picnicking facilities along the roads attract those who use the area for day use, the roads are the busiest part of the reserve. The backcountry, particularly to the north up the North Creek drainage, provides ample solitude and challenges. This drainage climbs up a narrow canyon from the basin floor, and the vegetation, primarily cedar, scrub oak, and sagebrush, becomes progressively denser.

The dense rock formations do not lend themselves to off-road use, so most of these enthusiasts pursue their sport in the more open and nearby Jim Sage Mountain area.

The City of Rocks Visitor Center is located in Almo, Idaho. Brochures, climbing guides, historic trail information, camping information, and community sharing exhibits (displays by local residents highlighting the history of the area) are offered here. Overnight camping permits are required in the reserve and are available here as well.

The City of Rocks Historical Association was formed to preserve the cultural and historical features of the reserve, as well as to disseminate that information to the public. Some of its projects include restoring an old cabin for an interpretive display and preserving evidence of wagon train crossings.

HOW TO GET THERE From Burley take South Overland Road/Idaho Highway 27 south 20 miles to Oakley. From Oakley take Birch Creek Road south 17 miles to Moulton.

California Trail: To access the California Trail take Birch Creek Road south from Oakley to the town of Moulton, 17 miles. Drive 2 miles east on the Twin Sisters/City of Rocks Road until you enter the reserve. There is no trailhead per se; access the historic California Trail route by parking at the turnoff immediately after entering the reserve. Walk due south approximately 100 feet, where you should be able to see the trail. The trail is wide (wagon-wide) and runs east–west for 1 mile, following the road.

Day Hike

California Trail

Distance: 10 miles round-trip.
Difficulty: Moderately easy.
Topo maps: Almo-ID; Cache Peak-ID.

Though this trail does not offer a lot of backcountry solitude, the opportunity to walk this historic trail should not be missed. The California Trail follows the route of the early pioneers as they made their way to the gold fields of the west. Wagon ruts are still visible and it is possible to find other artifacts, such as utensils and tools, along the route (these artifacts are protected by law and must be left undisturbed).

From the reserve boundary the trail follows the old wagon trail through the sagebrush and up a gradual 2.5 miles to Pinnacle Pass, where you will be able to view the Twin Sisters pinnacles on the left. Slightly more than 2 miles farther on, the trail and Twin Sisters/City of Rocks Road meet at Camp Rock. This huge piece of granite is a rounded and distinctive landmark on the trail. From this point the trail crosses Circle Creek and then exits the reserve after 1.5 miles. The trail then more closely follows the road on its way to Almo, 2 miles to the east.

Bruneau Dunes State Park

7

Location: Southern Idaho, 18 miles southwest of Mountain Home.
Size: 4,800 acres.
Administration: Idaho Department of Parks and Recreation.
Management status: Roadless.
Ecosystems: Intermountain semi-desert province; arid and characterized by sagebrush steppes and sand dunes; sagebrush and shad scale along with short grasses; contains several types of habitat, including lake, marsh, desert prairie, and dune.
Elevation range: 2,470 feet at Sand Dune Lakes to 3,077 feet at the dune peaks.
System trails: 6 miles.
Maximum core to perimeter distance: 5 miles.
Activities: Hiking, dune climbing, fishing, camping, and stargazing.
Best months: March and April.
Maps: Bruneau Dunes-ID (USGS 1:1,000,000); Bruneau Dunes Visitor's Map.

OVERVIEW Bruneau Dunes State Park contains some of the tallest, single-structured sand dunes in North America, towering to 470 feet and rising above two small lakes known as Sand Dune Lakes. According to a spokesperson at park headquarters, the lakes form one large body of water during the spring runoff and split into two separate lakes as the summer progresses. They are collectively referred to as Sand Dune Lakes. The lakes appeared in 1954 with the rise of the water table when reservoirs were formed on the Snake River; they offer excellent fishing for largemouth bass and bluegill.

The lakes are a powerful attraction in this arid region, with duck species and tundra swans, Canada geese, and great blue herons flocking to the place. Less common but still observable are American avocets, long-billed curlews, red-necked and Wilson's phalaropes, western and least sandpipers, black-necked stilts, and killdeer. Bruneau Dunes State Park is a part of the Snake River Birds of Prey National Conservation Area, and raptors, including golden eagles, can be viewed.

Due to the extreme daytime temperatures, resident mammals and reptiles are harder to view. These include coyote, black-tailed jackrabbit, Ord's kangaroo rat, short-horned and western whiptail lizard, and gopher snake.

The Dunes area is composed of salt and pepper sand of basalt and rhyolite grains, unique in the Western Hemisphere. The combination of a sand source, a relatively constant wind, and a natural trap has caused sand to collect in this

7   BRUNEAU DUNES STATE PARK

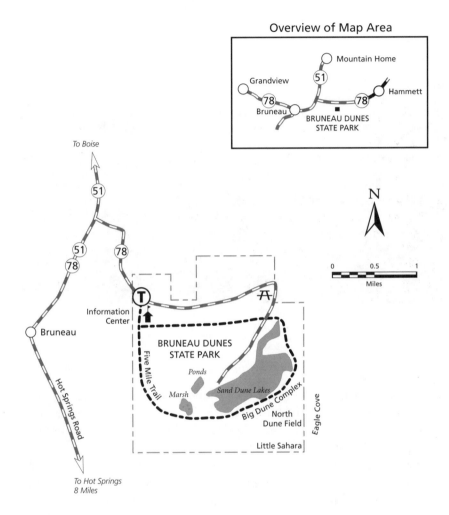

Overview of Map Area

semicircular basin for approximately 12,000 years. Unlike most dunes, these don't drift far; the prevailing winds blow from the southeast 28 percent of the time and from the northwest 32 percent of the time, thus keeping the dunes relatively stable. The two most prominent dunes cover 600 acres.

The Bruneau area is also noteworthy because of one of its tiniest inhabitants: *Pyrgulopsis Bruneauensis*, better known as the Bruneau Hot Springs Snail. These snails—currently on the endangered species list—measure less than ⅛ inch long and populate the nearby hot springs.

Idaho's version of the Sahara Desert includes North America's largest dune.

RECREATIONAL USES A comprehensive visitor information center and museum are located at the Bruneau Dunes entrance. Stop and pick up the interpretive map for the main park trail, which details the diverse desert animals and plant life in the area. The map gives tips on how to locate and identify the many species of animals found at the dunes.

The park maintains camping facilities east of the visitors center. A separate picnic area lies to the south, close to the lake and dunes. Camping, boating (nonmotorized), fishing, and hiking are the main recreational activities at Bruneau Dunes. Typical sand dune activity—rolling, sliding, tubing, and sand skiing—is irresistible off the top of the dunes. All motorized vehicles are prohibited and the law is strictly enforced.

The park is in an isolated location and therefore has no "light pollution." This fact, and the fact that it is located fairly close to the city of Boise, makes it a popular destination for amateur as well as professional astronomers. The Bruneau Dunes State Park Observatory is open to the public; call the park headquarters for the hours of operation. In addition, the Boise Astronomical Society holds an annual "Star Party" on the third Saturday in August. Telescopes are set up, and members of the society help the public view the stars and learn about astronomy.

HOW TO GET THERE From Boise travel 42 miles east on I–84, then take exit 90, Mountain Home. Travel southwest 15 miles on Idaho Highway 51, then east on Idaho Highway 78 for 2 miles to the Snake River. Pick up a guide to the park at the visitors center. There is a camping fee.

Day Hike

Five Mile Trail

Distance: 5-mile loop.
Difficulty: Moderate.
Topo map: Bruneau Dunes Visitor's Map.

The Big Dune complex appears to be one large dune, but it is actually two dunes that join and form a small crater at their junction. These dunes form a dramatic backdrop to Sand Dune Lakes. This trail takes three to six hours to walk and follows the ridgeline of the dunes, and then goes down along the shoreline of Sand Dune Lakes.

There are eight marker posts that define the trail identified on the Bruneau Dunes Visitor's Map. Posts 1 through 3 guide you around the marsh. From Post 3 you can walk straight to the crest of the big sand dune. At this point you are 470 feet above the lake and have an excellent view of the surrounding desert. Upon leaving the top the trail follows the crest down to the shoreline and Post 5. Post 6 is at the crossroads and 7 and 8 bring you back to your starting point. The map provides useful information on wildlife and geology that coincides with the trail markers.

Though this is not a wilderness area, few people venture very far in this desert climate, and fewer still hike the trail. Since daytime temperatures can reach 110 degrees F, attempt the trail in the early morning or later evening hours. These are also the best times to view the varied animal species that inhabit the area. Still, remember to pack plenty of water.

Day or Overnight Hike

Overland Hike

Distance: Variable.
Difficulty: Moderate.
Topo maps: Bruneau Dunes-ID; Bruneau Dunes Visitor's Map.

Besides the main dune area (referred to as the Big Dune complex) that is serviced by the visitors center and campgrounds, there are several other areas worth exploring. North Dune Field, the "Little Sahara," and the rim of Eagle Cove provide excellent hiking opportunities. (Directions to these features can be obtained from the park ranger.) Be advised, though, that there is no designated trail system and that carrying an accurate topographic map and compass is advised. Also, keep in mind that there is no water available in these areas: You must carry an ample supply with you.

Immediately to the south of the Big Dune complex and 2.5 miles from the visitors center by the Five Mile Trail, is the North Dune Field. This area is characterized by numerous smaller dunes that are anchored by desert vegetation.

Lying southeast of the North Dune Field is the area called by local residents the "Little Sahara." This area offers the truest wilderness experience because its terrain and harsh climate discourage casual visitors. The hiker who ventures into Little Sahara will be rewarded by a wide variety of dune structures and geologically interesting features such as oases, playas, wadis, hammadas, and desert pavement.

Eagle Cove is the semicircular basin that the Bruneau Sand Dunes lie in. It is a massive sand trap that was formed by the Snake River when its ancient course followed this route. A hike following the rim of the Cove offers spectacular views of the entire park system.

Snake River Birds of Prey National Conservation Area

8

Location: Southwest Idaho, 35 miles south of Boise.
Size: 483,000 acres.
Administration: BLM, National Conservation Area.
Management status: Multiuse, with roadless areas.
Ecosystems: Great Plains/Palouse dry steppe province characterized by semi-arid, rolling plateaus cut by deep river canyons and dominated by extensive grasslands; this steppe is comprised of short grasses usually bunched and sparsely distributed, allowing for much soil exposure.
Elevation range: 2,625 feet at river bottom to 3,304 feet at Fossil Butte.
System trails: 10 miles.
Maximum core to perimeter distance: 10 miles.
Activities: Nature study, hiking, fishing, horseback riding, rafting, and boating.
Best months: March and April.
Maps: Coyote Butte-ID; Sinker Butte-ID; Wild Horse Butte-ID; Castle Butte-ID; Jackass Butte-ID; Dorsey Butte-ID; Vinson Wash-ID; Grand View-ID (USGS 1:1,000,000); Snake River Birds of Prey National Conservation Area, BLM.

OVERVIEW The Snake River Birds of Prey National Conservation Area (NCA) was established by Congress in 1993 to recognize and perpetuate the area's unique wildlife values. Crags and crevices, the deep canyon of the Snake River, thermal updrafts, and a broad plateau rich in small wildlife provide habitat for one of the greatest concentration of nesting birds of prey in North America—and perhaps the world. The Snake River Birds of Prey NCA—the only NCA in Idaho—is managed by the BLM.

The NCA encompasses 483,000 acres of public land along 81 miles of the Snake River in southwest Idaho. The river lies within a deep canyon that is surrounded by an expansive plateau. Cliffs towering up to 700 feet above the river provide countless ledges, cracks, and crevices for nesting birds of prey, also known as raptors.

At first glance the surrounding plateau seems unremarkable, but it holds the key that makes this area so valuable for birds of prey. During the past 10,000 years, desert winds have deposited a deep layer of finely textured soil on the north side of the Snake River Canyon. This soil and the plants that grow in it, including buffalo grass, sunflower, locoweed, grama, wheatgrass, and needlegrass, support large populations of ground squirrels and jackrabbits, the main food source for birds of prey.

8   SNAKE RIVER BIRDS OF PREY NATIONAL CONSERVATION AREA

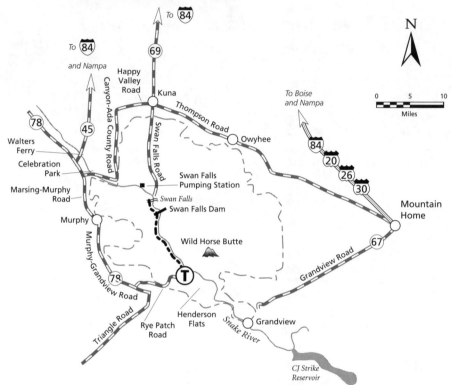

The combination of ideal and isolated nesting habitat in the Snake River Canyon and extraordinary prey habitat on the adjacent plateau make this a place like no other for these birds. The area's ecosystem acts as a natural raptor nursery, providing nesting opportunities for more than fifteen raptor species each spring. In addition nine other raptor species use the area during part of their annual migration.

More than a gathering spot for raptors, the NCA hosts one of the nation's largest concentrations of badgers and is one of the few places in Idaho to see black-throated sparrows. Approximately 260 wildlife species inhabit the area, including 45 mammals, 165 birds, 8 amphibians, 16 reptiles, and 25 fish. This variety of species caused the entire NCA to be designated as a Watchable Wildlife Area.

RECREATIONAL USES Most of the Snake River Birds of Prey roadless area is surrounded by the NCA, which allows for multi-use access (this includes motorized vehicles). Don't let this discourage you from the trip, though.

The NCA provides opportunities for many types of recreationists, and little of the area has been designated as nonmotorized. In fact just 4.5 miles of the Snake River Canyon north of the river—from the Initial Butte Farm's pump station downstream to the Canyon County line—is designated as such.

With these facts in mind, you *can* plan to see these raptors in their natural habitat without disturbance. One way is to drop down into the canyon at the Initial Butte Farm's pump station and follow the nonmotorized section of the Snake River to the Canyon County line. However, you can also find good, solitary sidetrips along the Snake River upriver as far as the town of Grand View. The town of Swan Falls, within this section, also has a good put-in for river trips using kayaks or canoes. Be aware, too, that the fishing is excellent throughout this section of the Snake River, and you may encounter anglers along the banks downriver of Swan Falls (though not upriver).

HOW TO GET THERE *Wild Horse Butte:* Take I–84 (15 miles south of Boise) to exit 44 (Meridian). From Meridian travel 8 miles south on Idaho Highway 69 to the town of Kuna. From Kuna take Kuna Road west for 5 miles to Happy Valley Road. Here you make a left, heading south. This road becomes Canyon-Ada County Road at the intersection with Bowmont Road (approximately 2 miles). Continue south on Canyon-Ada County Road 18 miles to the town of Murphy (you'll cross the Snake River). From Murphy take Idaho Highway 78 for 7 miles. At this point there is an unimproved road to the left (north); follow it for approximately 9 miles. The trail begins at the end of this road.

Swan Falls Dam: Put-in: Take Swan Falls Road from Kuna to the dam. Take-out: From Kuna take I–84 to Nampa. Here you take Idaho Highway 45 south to the river. Directly after crossing the Snake River there will be a boat ramp turn-off on the right side for the take-out at Walters Ferry.

Day Hike

Wild Horse Butte to Swan Falls

Distance: 12 miles one way.
Difficulty: Easy.
Topo map: Snake River Birds of Prey trail map

This trail follows the Snake River from Wild Horse Butte to Swan Falls. From the end of the road (there is no trailhead) it is a 1-mile walk to the river, past the Wild Horse Butte on your right (east). Though there is no designated trail at this point, you simply head downstream and follow the river northwest as it flows toward the town of Swan Falls.

The Birds of Prey Center is a valuable introduction to the management area.

This section is designated as multi-use, but there are no roads, unimproved or otherwise, to access the river; the opportunity for bird-watching in solitude is therefore exceptional.

Several feeder streams flow into the river along this route, so fishing for native trout species is terrific.

River Trip

Swan Falls Dam to Walters Ferry

Distance: 14 river miles.
Difficulty: Easy to moderate.
Topo map: Snake River Birds of Prey trail map

This trip allows for bird-watching from the water and contains moderate white water on a very wide river. Class I to Class II water predominates in moderate stream flows with no notable hazards. The put-in is just below the Swan Falls Dam and take-out is at Walters Ferry.

Be sure to bring binoculars, so you can observe the raptors; there are also Indian petroglyphs on some canyon walls. Celebration Park, 10 miles downstream on the right-hand side, has a very good museum and is worth a stop.

Bruneau–Jarbridge River Area   9

Location: Southwest Idaho, 12 miles south of Bruneau.
Size: 350,000 acres.
Administration: BLM, Special Recreaton Management Area (SRMA).
Management status: Roadless, wilderness study area (43,100 acres managed by the BLM).
Ecosystems: Great Plains Palouse dry steppe province characterized by semi-arid, rolling plateaus cut by deep river canyons and dominated by extensive grasslands; this steppe is comprised of short grasses usually bunched and sparsely distributed, allowing for much soil exposure.
Elevation range: 3,785 feet at Big Draw to 5,676 feet at Poison Butte.
System trails: 129 miles, which includes 75 miles of designated trail, the Idaho State Centennial Trail.
Maximum core to perimeter distance: 16 miles.
Activities: Hiking, mountain biking, and kayaking.
Best months: March and April.
Maps: Hot Spring-ID; Broken Wagon Flat-ID; Crowbar Gulch-ID; Pot Hole Butte-ID; Table Butte-ID; Austin Butte-ID; Winter Camp-ID; Hodge Station-ID; Cave Draw-ID; Stiff Tree Draw-ID; Clover Butte North-ID; Indian Hot Springs-ID; Inside Lakes-ID; Clover Butte South-ID; Triguero Lake-ID; The Arch-ID; Poison Butte-ID; Mosquito Lake Butte-ID; Cowan Reservoir-ID; Dishpan-ID; Murphy Hot Spring-ID (USGS 1:1,000,000); BLM Bruneau–Jarbridge River Guide.

OVERVIEW The Bruneau–Jarbridge ("brown" and "devil" in French) River Area is as isolated a place as you can find in the United States. Driving south from the town of Bruneau, you enter a world characterized by seemingly endless desert. The horizon is limitless and disorienting with virtually no visual landmarks. However, this featureless plain is cut through with spectacular steep-walled canyons that drop as much as 1200 feet deep. The area is little known and little used and accessed by only a few remote roads. The BLM currently has the area under its Special Recreation Management Area (SRMA) designation and is considering it for wilderness designation.

The major attraction of this area, and the challenge, is the rivers, as they offer exceptional white-water canoeing, rafting, and kayaking in a primitive and isolated setting. The Bruneau and Jarbridge originate in Nevada's Humbolt National Forest and the Jarbridge Wilderness and flow north into Idaho where they join east of Grasmere. These rivers provide great whitewater in the spring runoff months of April and early May and provide a more serene—and

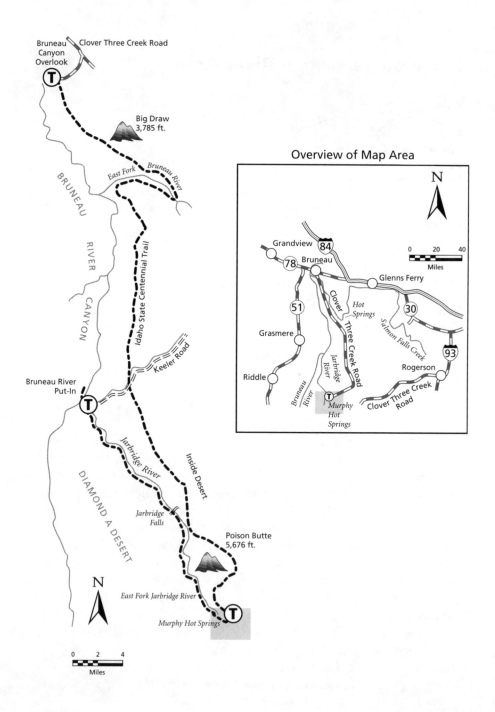

less challenging—experience as the water level drops by the end of June (thus offering access for people of all skill levels).

The surrounding desert supports many species of grasses, including buffalo grass, sunflower, and locoweed, all common to this area. Other grasses include grama, wheatgrass, and needlegrass. These extensive and nutritious grasslands were an important part of the range of the large herds of buffalo that grazed the Great Plains in the early 1900s. Though the buffalo are gone, it is easy to envision them wandering these vast plains. Today, the pronghorn antelope and the mule deer are the most common big-game species. Smaller mammals include jackrabbit, coyote, and numerous rodent species.

RECREATIONAL USES This area is extremely remote and little used. The high-country desert holds little attraction for cattle ranchers, and minerals, gas, and oil have not been found in enough quantities to make extraction profitable. Couple these limitations with the fact that there are few water sources and you have a prescription for continued isolation. The area's major use comes from the Mountain Home Air Force Base, which has access to land east of the Bruneau Canyon in the Saylor Creek Air Force Range. This area is so vast that you are aware of the base's existence only by signs at isolated road crossings.

River use peaks in early April when the water level is at its highest. The region's imposing expanse of seemingly endless desert has discouraged casual hikers from making forays into the area. However, hiking opportunities are here and can easily provide a pure wilderness experience without the distraction of civilization. Opportunities are limited only by the accuracy of your maps and the amount of water you can carry. There is only one designated trail in this vast desert, so care should be taken when venturing off the access roads.

HOW TO GET THERE *Jarbridge River:* From Bruneau take Hot Springs Road to Hot Springs, 7 miles. Take Clover Three Creek Road heading southeast from Hot Springs for 27 miles. At this point take the fork of the road headed due south and continue for another 30 miles. Here you will access Clover Three Creek Road by turning right (southwest). Continue 6 miles to Murphy Hot Springs.

Idaho State Centennial Trail: Travel 8 miles south from Hot Springs. Turn west (right) to the Bruneau Canyon overlook and the trail access (there is no trailhead and the trail is seldom marked; accurate topo maps and compass are recommended).

Overnight Kayak Trip

Jarbridge River

Distance: 25 miles one way.
Difficulty: Moderately strenuous; primarily Class III waters.
Topo maps: Indian Hot Springs-ID; Inside Lakes-ID; The Arch-ID; Poison Butte-ID; Dishpan-ID; Murphy Hot Spring-ID; BLM Bruneau–Jarbridge River Guide.

The Jarbridge River is becoming a quiet mecca for kayakers because of its beauty, classic white water, and total isolation. However, be very confident of your skills and your craft, and be prepared for wilderness travel. This includes extensive pre-trip planning, knowing the river, and letting others know your plans.

The put-in for this trip is at Murphy Hot Springs; follow the Jarbridge north until it joins with the Bruneau River. The take-out at Indian Hot Springs is less than a mile downriver from the confluence of the two rivers.

The river is relatively easy to negotiate in most places and is typically attempted in early April when the water level is at its highest. At this time of year the water is fast and provides good white-water action; there is just one portage, at Jarbridge Falls. Late spring travel is much slower as the water level drops and more rocks are exposed; water travel becomes impossible as summer progresses. Sage brush, cedar, and juniper predominate on the floor of the canyon, and there are many suitable camping spots available. Use caution as rattlesnakes and poison ivy are common along much of the river.

Extended Overnight Hike

Idaho State Centennial Trail

Distance: 62 miles.
Difficulty: Strenuous.
Topo maps: Hot Spring-ID; Crowbar Gulch-ID; Pot Hole Butte-ID; Austin Butte-ID; Winter Camp-ID; Cave Draw-ID; Stiff Tree Draw-ID; Indian Hot Springs-ID; Inside Lakes-ID; Triguero Lake-ID; The Arch-ID; Poison Butte-ID; Mosquito Lake Butte-ID; Cowan Reservoir-ID; Dishpan-ID; Murphy Hot Spring-ID; BLM Bruneau–Jarbridge River Guide.

For those who want the ultimate backcountry wilderness experience, this trip is for you. This section of the historic Idaho State Centennial Trail will provide you with a solitude that can only be described as profound. The trail is part of the 1,200-mile hike that stretches through Idaho from the Nevada border to Canada. And at this southernmost section of the trail, there are sweeping vistas of the high-country desert and virtually no opportunity to encounter another human being. The hike is not technically difficult as the land offers little topographical change. However, due to the desert conditions, length of the hike, and few visual landmarks, adequate preparation is crucial before attempting the hike. Plan the trip for early spring when feeder streams will be running.

The trail has dead-end feeder roads accessing it at intervals of approximately every 4 to 6 miles. In planning the trip, consider having someone meet you at a predesignated feeder road to restock or cache supplies.

Thirteen miles into the hike the trail will cross the East Fork of the Bruneau River and cut due west for 5 miles before continuing its southern progress. All along the route intermittent streams cross the trail and may provide access to water dependent on the time of year.

Approximately 19 miles from the East Fork crossing, the trail will connect with a feeder road heading southwest. It's worth a side trip to follow this road 3 miles to the confluence of the Bruneau and Jarbridge Rivers. Backtracking to the trail, you will roughly follow the Jarbridge River for 12 miles before detouring around the 5,676-foot-tall Poison Butte. The trail then drops back and closely follows the Jarbridge (now it's East Fork) into the town of Murphy Hot Springs.

Owyhee River Canyonlands

10

Location: Southwest Idaho, 90 miles southwest of Boise.
Size: 333,000 acres.
Administration: BLM, SRMA.
Management status: Roadless, nonwilderness.
Ecosystems: Intermountain semidesert and desert province characterized by semi-arid, sagebrush-covered plateaus cut by deep river canyons and dominated by extensive grasslands; this sagebrush steppe is comprised of short grasses usually bunched and sparsely distributed, allowing for much soil exposure.
Elevation range: 5,140 feet at the Little Owyhee River to 6,775 feet at Juniper Mountain.
System trails: No designated trails.
Maximum core to perimeter distance: 40 miles.
Activities: Hiking, floating, kayaking, and canoeing.
Best months: March and April.
Maps: Bedstead Ridge-ID; Smith Creek-ID; Castro Table-ID; Dickshooter Reservoir-ID; Frying Pan Basin-ID; Lost Valley-ID; Bull Basin Camp-ID; Red Basin-ID; Brace Flat-ID; Dickshooter Ridge-ID; Battle Creek Lakes-ID; Shoofly Springs-ID; Nichol Flat-ID; Spring Creek Basin-ID; Grassy Ridge-ID; Piute Basin West-ID; Jarvis Pasture-ID; Ross Lake-ID; Flying H Ranch-ID; Star Valley-ID; Coyote Hole-ID; Bull Camp Butte-ID; Four Corners-ID; Juniper Basin-ID; Juniper Basin SE-ID; Mountain View Lake-ID; Three Forks-ID (USGS 1:1,000,000).

OVERVIEW Rising from its headwaters in the high desert of Nevada, Idaho, and Oregon, the Owyhee River and its tributaries cut a stunning complex of deep, steep-walled canyons through the plateaus and mesas of the area. The Owyhee River Canyonlands was named for a group of Hawaiians who disappeared up the river in 1810. "Owyhee," a phonetic spelling of Hawaii, is currently unprotected. It is one of the largest such wild areas in the lower forty-eight states.

Due to its unprotected status, Owyhee has a few primitive roads, and cattle grazing is allowed. However, due to the immensity of this region and the generally poor forage opportunities, grazing is minimal. The spectacular canyons and mesa wilderness easily offer the type of outdoor experience that can be classified as "wild." The canyons, white-water desert rivers, and vast plateaus of the Canyonlands are part of the Great Basin ecosystem, though they also continue into the Snake River Plateau. The elevation range within the complex spans from more than 9,000 feet in Nevada's Jarbridge Wilderness to 4,000 feet at the level of the Owyhee River in Idaho. This diversity encourages

10A OWYHEE RIVER CANYONLANDS (OVERVIEW)

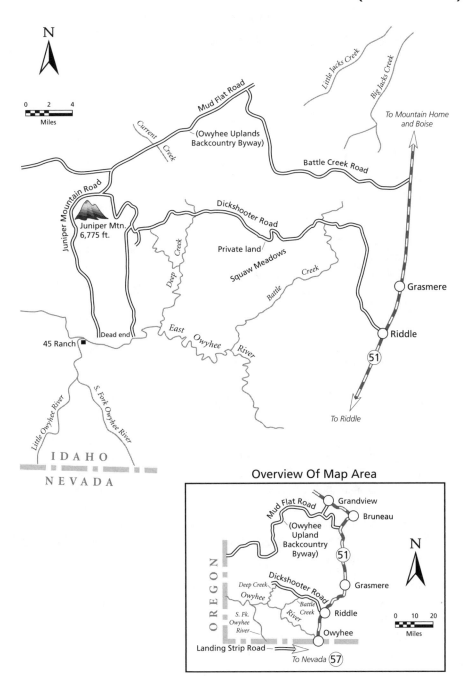

Overview Of Map Area

10B OWYHEE RIVER CANYONLANDS (OWYHEE UPLANDS NATIONAL BACKCOUNTRY BYWAY)

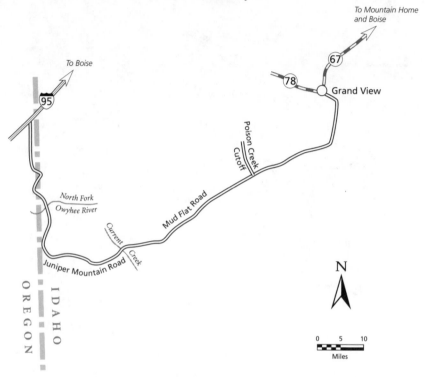

the survival of various rare and threatened species, including the California desert bighorn sheep. Other common desert animal species include the peregrine falcon, cougar, bobcat, sage grouse, redband trout, beaver, otter, pronghorn antelope, mule deer, and coyote. These species thrive in part because of the remoteness and inaccessibility of the region, as well as the nutritious grasses that grow here. These include buffalo grass, sunflower, locoweed, grama, wheatgrass, and needlegrass.

RECREATIONAL USES Recreational use of the rivers in the Owyhee Canyonlands is growing as more and more rafters and boaters are running these spectacular high-desert rivers. Be aware, though, that the Upper Owyhee is contained within a narrow canyon and offers technical white water, appropriate only for expert users. The Middle Owyhee widens out of the canyon and contains more water and bigger waves, still a place for experts. The Lower Owyhee is appropriate for many skill levels, according to stream flows. Here

The isolation of these lands south of Boise is a large part of the attraction.

the Owyhee has left the canyon and the water is somewhat more sedate. The East and South Forks are more navigable by intermediate users.

The Big and Little Jacks Creek Canyons offer outstanding opportunities for hiking, and hunters have ample opportunity to track bighorn sheep, mule deer, and pronghorn antelope. Subsequently, these canyons see the most use by visitors. Hiking opportunities abound in the remainder of this vast region due to the absence of significant roads, though there are very few designated hiking trails. Exploration of the extensive river system and the intermittent lake and stream beds can be the goal of endless backcountry hikes. High-quality topographic maps and a good compass can lead you to a truly unique hiking experience within the Owyhee River Canyonlands.

What makes the Canyonlands so unique—the vast desolation—has drawn the interest of the U.S. Department of Defense. Its proposal is to include this area in an aerial bombing range that would be an extension of the range currently in use by the Mountain Home Air Force Base adjacent to the Bruneau–Jarbridge Area (see chapter 9 for more information). The Wilderness Society has been combating this proposal, which includes up to three million acres of public land in southwest Idaho, Oregon, and Nevada. Of particular concern to the opponents of the proposal is the noise from overhead aircraft, which would disturb recreationists and marginal species in the area, thus possibly decreasing the animals' chances for survival.

HOW TO GET THERE *South Fork Owyhee River:* From Mountain City, Nevada, take Nevada Highway 51 north to the town of Owyhee, also in Nevada. From Owyhee travel due west on Landing Strip Road approximately 25 miles to the put-in at South Fork Pipeline in Nevada. The access to the water is very steep and may require four-wheel-drive in wet conditions.

The take-out is at the 45 Ranch in Idaho at the confluence of the East and South Forks of the Owyhee River.

Owyhee Uplands National Backcountry Byway: The trip starts 3 miles south of Grand View, Idaho. Grand View is located 23 miles southwest of Mountain Home on Idaho Highway 67. The route proceeds southwest to its final destination at Jordan Valley, Oregon.

River Trip

South Fork Owyhee River

Distance: 22 miles one way.
Difficulty: Moderately strenuous.
Topo maps: Owyhee River map available from the BLM Owyhee Field Office; see Appendix C for contact information.

This section of the Owyhee is a good introduction to the river for intermediate users. The river flows through a beautiful desert canyon with sheer walls and occasional rock spires. This trip is typically run in spring and early summer with white water classed at III and IV. Putting-in at different stream flows will make the trip appropriate for rafts, kayaks, or canoes. This section of the Owyhee is classified as a Wild and Scenic river.

Put-in is at South Fork Pipeline, Nevada, and the take-out is at 45 Ranch in Idaho. The shuttle back to the put-in will take approximately eight to twelve hours.

Camping is allowed, with restrictions, and permits are required before running the river.

Road Trip

Owyhee Uplands National Backcountry Byway

Distance: 145-mile loop.
Difficulty: Moderate in dry weather, impassable when wet.
Topo map: Route map available from the BLM Owyhee Field Office; see Appendix C for contact information.

Another option for checking out this country is to access the Owyhee Uplands National Backcountry Byway. This is a lengthy road trip that is a good introduction to the wonders of the area, including a great overlook of the North Fork of the Owyhee.

The trip takes approximately eight hours on dry road; it is impassable in wet conditions. There are no services along the route and virtually no traffic, so it's advisable to bring adequate supplies, including water, as well as a full tank of gas. For these reasons as well as the road's few blind curves and grades in excess of 10 degrees, the trip rates moderate.

The scenery includes expansive high desert and attractive mesas. On approaching the North Fork of the Owyhee River, you will get a fantastic view of its sheer, redrock canyon walls. There is a nice campground near this overlook. As the route turns north and crisscrosses in and out of Oregon, you will enter western juniper woodlands; some of these trees are estimated to be more than 500 years old. The route ends at Jordan Valley; I–95 will take you north back toward Boise, Idaho.

North-Central:
Frank Church/Sawtooth/Selway

Frank Church–River of No Return Wilderness Area

11

Location: Central Idaho, 37 miles north of Stanley.
Size: 2,373,321 acres.
Administration: USDAFS, Bitterroot, Boise, Challis, Nez Perce, Payette, and Salmon National Forests.
Management status: Wilderness.
Ecosystems: Middle Rocky Mountain coniferous forest/alpine meadow province, Idaho Batholith section, characterized by strongly glaciated mountains with cirques and U-shaped valleys; Douglas fir, western spruce-fir, and western ponderosa forest types, many perennial streams and higher-elevation lakes.
Elevation range: 1,920 feet at Wind River pack bridge to 10,442 feet at White Mountain.
System trails: 2,720 miles of trails originating from sixty-six trailheads.
Maximum core to perimeter distance: 65 miles.
Activities: Hiking, horseback riding, hunting, fishing, and white-water rafting.
Maps: 1996 Frank Church–River of No Return Wilderness Area Forest Service topographic maps, North and South. (Due to the large number of maps covering this area, see Appendix D for a full listing of the USGS 1:1,000,000 maps covering the complex.)

OVERVIEW The Frank Church–River of No Return Wilderness Area is the largest wilderness area in the lower forty-eight states and the largest administered by the Forest Service. The River of No Return Wilderness was created by Congress with the passage of the Central Idaho Wilderness Act on July 23, 1980. Frank Church's name was added to the wilderness in 1983, one month before his death. Church, an Idahoan senator, was a key figure in the creation of this wilderness and the passage of the 1964 Wilderness Act and the Wild and Scenic Rivers bill in 1968. He is quoted as saying: "I never knew a man who felt self-important in the morning after spending the night in the open on an Idaho mountain-side under a star-studded summer sky. Save some time in your lives for the outdoors, where you can be witness to the wonders of God."

Most of the area lies within the drainage of the Salmon River and its tributaries, encompassing an area 90 miles long and 56 miles wide. The Salmon River and its three branches are so imposing that they thwarted the first attempt of the Lewis and Clark expedition to find a river route to the Pacific Ocean. The expedition made their attempt near present-day Shoup, Idaho, on the main Salmon. The rivers within the wilderness are so remote and so valu-

11A FRANK CHURCH–RIVER OF NO RETURN WILDERNESS AREA (OVERVIEW)

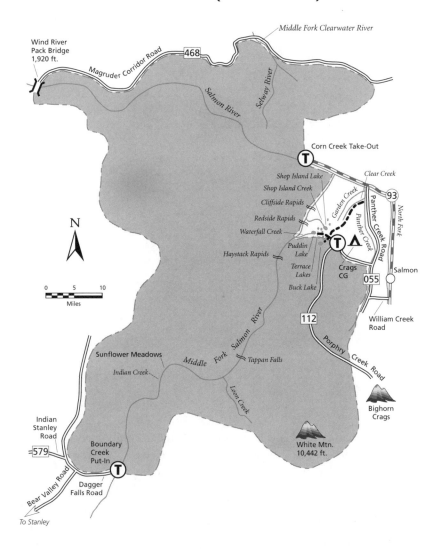

able that just more than 200 miles of them have been designated Wild and Scenic Rivers (106 miles of the Middle Fork of the Salmon River, 77 miles of the main Salmon, and 18 miles of the upper Selway). The main Salmon River has formed an enormous gorge that constitutes the second deepest gorge in the continental United States, and due to its location in the center of the complex, no road approaches the canyon for 80 miles. These rivers are fed by deep winter snows and more than 400 lakes that are studded throughout the area.

11B FRANK CHURCH–RIVER OF NO RETURN
WILDERNESS AREA (BIGHORN CRAG AREA)

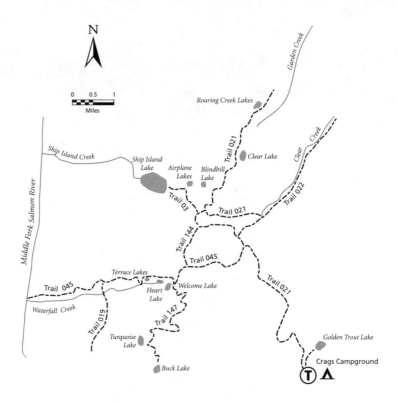

The immensity of this wilderness is difficult to comprehend. From the air the rugged and heavily forested mountains stretch past the horizon and periodically drop away into the deep canyons formed by the powerful rivers. The forest consists primarily of Douglas fir, with stands of ponderosa and lodgepole pine, Engelmann spruce, subalpine fir, and western larch. Numerous peaks within the Frank Church exceed 10,000 feet; at this elevation the terrain is windswept and very sheer. For the most part, below 7,500 feet the terrain is thick with vegetation and somewhat more accommodating to overland travel. The Chamberlain Basin is a unique area within the wilderness. It is located between the Main and South Salmon Canyons and is a vast, high plateau that is primarily flat and dotted with meadows. Due to the size and steep terrain contained within the Frank Church, most of the area is lightly traveled despite the fact that there are more than 2,500 miles of excellent trails.

The area's ecological diversity and its isolation promotes a rich and varied home for over 370 wildlife species. Large mammals are plentiful and many are easily observed. These include mule and white-tailed deer, elk, moose, bighorn sheep, mountain lion, black bear, and mountain goat. Grizzlies, lynx, coyote, fox, and wolverine also find prime habitat within the wilderness. Fish are also varied and plentiful and include Chinook salmon; steelhead, cutthroat, bull (Dolly Varden), rainbow, brook, and golden trout; and arctic grayling. The main Salmon is one of the primary spawning grounds for the Chinook salmon and steelhead trout.

RECREATIONAL USES Due to the immensity of the Frank Church–River of No Return, most areas cannot be accessed without planning an extended trip. Day and overnight hikes are possible on the east, south, and west sides by trails originating from Forest Service roads serving the area. Access from the north is by trailheads along the Magruder Corridor road and by rafting or jet boating (allowed on the main Salmon) along the Salmon River. Cross-country skiing is possible along the fringes of the wilderness area.

Access to the extreme backcountry is limited to tiny and remote airstrips, horseback riding, extended hikes, and white-water rafting. The airstrips are available because several isolated, private landholdings were grandfathered in to the wilderness with its designation. These are accessible only via permit.

Though the area is rugged, the trails are well maintained, and many do not contain extreme elevation changes. Several nationally designated trails travel through the Frank Church, including the Continental Divide National Scenic Trail, Lewis and Clark National Historic Trail, and the Nee Me Poo National Historic Trail. Pack trips with horses are an excellent way to access the remote backcountry. Float trips down the branches of the Salmon River are very popular and account for the bulk of day use visitors. Depending on the season and water flow, some of these floats are appropriate for less-experienced travelers. The Forest Service can provide detailed trip and condition reports; permits are required. Backcountry hunting and fishing trips to the Salmon River and its tributaries are also big draws into the area, and many commercial outfitters offer a variety of options.

HOW TO GET THERE *Middle Fork of the Salmon River:* The put-in spot to float the Middle Fork of the Salmon River is at the end of Dagger Falls Road at Boundary Creek. Take Idaho Highway 21 north from Stanley for 20 miles. Turn left on Bear Valley Road as it leads west. Travel 9 miles, and then turn right (north) onto Dagger Falls Road. From there it's 8 miles to several campsites and the put-in for the river. Arrangements must be made to be picked up at the Corn Creek take-out on the main Salmon River: Take U.S. Highway 93 north from Salmon for 15 miles until you reach the town of North Fork. Turn left toward Shoup and follow the river 47 miles until you reach the Corn Creek take-out.

Bighorn Crags/Buck Lake: The Bighorn Crags area is accessed by traveling 5 miles south from Salmon on U.S. Highway 93 to Willams Creek Road. Willams Creek Road climbs west into the forest for 12 miles where it turns into Panther

The Salmon River near Shoup. Nearby is the northeastern point of the Frank Church–River of No Return Wilderness as well as the point where the Lewis and Clark party decided to seek an alternative route.

Creek Road, Forest Road 055. From there turn right on Forest Road 112, Porphyry Creek, and travel 6 miles. At this point you leave the good road for one that is a little more rugged and which heads north (Forest Road 113). This road will take you 8 miles to the Crags Campground, which has full facilities and charges a fee. The campground is open from about July 10 through mid-October.

Extended Raft Trip

Middle Fork of the Salmon River

Distance: 120 river miles one way (five days).
Difficulty: Strenuous.
Topo maps: Middle Fork of the Salmon River available from the Middle Fork Ranger District, Challis (detailed map of each running mile includes rapids information); Bull Trout Point-ID; Bule Bunch Mtn.-ID; Cape Horn Lakes-ID; Big Soldier Mtn.-ID; Soldier Creek-ID; Artillery Dome-ID; Little Soldier Mtn.-ID; Pungo Mtn.-ID; Norton Ridge-ID; Sliderock Ridge-ID; Ramey Hill-ID; Aparejo Mtn.-ID; Puddin Mtn.-ID; Aggipah Mtn.-ID; Butts Creek Point-ID; Long Tom Mtn.-ID.

It's approximately 120 river miles from Boundary Creek to the take-out at Corn Creek on the main Salmon River. During the spring runoff, late May through June, when water levels can reach 9 feet, this trip can take four days. As the water level drops to 3 feet in late season, mid-August and early September, the trip may take as much as two full days longer to complete. Late season travel and lower water flows also reduce the classification of existing rapids, while exposing more rocks within the riverbed.

Check with the Middle Fork Ranger District in the Challis National Forest before undertaking this trip, as permits are required. The ranger district will assign your campsites as well as alert you to any hazards on the river. It is critical to obtain and study the appropriate maps for this area. The Middle Fork of the Salmon River contains Class V white water, and you should be prepared to portage around these rapids if your equipment or skills are not adequate for the conditions.

The campsites are excellent and set almost exclusively on fine, white-sand beaches. Bio-toilets, self-contained and prepackaged for easy removal of waste, are required as few outdoor toilets are available; and, of those that are, some are being dismantled to preserve the primitive aspect of the river. The Middle Fork of the Salmon River must be considered a model of wilderness management. The Forest Service has been aggressive in patrolling and maintaining this resource, and it educates each user as to the "river rules." An estimated 10,000 people float this river every year, yet there is virtually no trace of their passage.

Though there is traffic on the river from other rafts, it is not unusual to enjoy the river in complete solitude, particularly in the late season. Hiking from one of the campsites on the numerous trails that access the river allows for back-country isolation, too, and there are a number of easily accessible hot springs.

The Middle Fork starts off at an elevation of 5,800 feet at Boundary Creek, with fairly mild rapids (dependent on the time of year), and the white water gets progressively more technical down river as the elevation drops to the Corn Creek take-out (at an elevation of 3,000 feet). From Boundary Creek the country is rugged and covered with evergreens clinging to the steep walls of the canyon. Evidence of old homesteader cabins still exist in the canyon, and several that have been grandfathered in are still maintained and lived in. Three primitive airstrips also exist in the canyon.

Several hot springs flow into the river and make for an enjoyable midday stop; Sunflower Meadows is a great example (it lies below the Indian Creek airstrip). Sunflower Meadows is a series of four shallow pools with temperatures ranging from tepid to scalding. A day farther and 11 river miles downstream, you'll encounter Loon Creek emptying into the river on the right side; there is a good hot pool by trail access 1 mile up the creek.

Three days into the trip the canyon walls become even steeper, and there is less vegetation. The river carves a path through the granite and the rapids become increasingly faster and more technical. Haystack, Red Cliff, and Redside rapids provide increasing white-water challenge. Here you will find evidence of the Sheepeater band of Shoshone Indians who made the river their home. The tribe left numerous petroglyphs in deep caves along the river, as well as smoke stains on the rocks from cooking fires. Their main source of meat was the bighorn sheep, which can frequently be seen grazing on the sheer cliff faces.

The river widens slightly as it nears its spill out into the main Salmon below the town of Shoup. This is the area where the Lewis and Clark party decided, on the wise advice of their Lemhi Indian guides, to detour north through Montana and attempt to cross Idaho at Lolo Pass. Mountain goats are numerous here along the canyon walls and are easily spotted from the river. From Shoup it's a mild 3-mile ride to the take-out at Corn Creek.

Day or Overnight Hike

Bighorn Crags/Buck Lake

Distance: 13 miles round-trip.
Difficulty: Strenuous.
Topo maps: Long Tom Mtn.-ID; Big Horn Crags-ID; Aggipah Mtn.-ID; Mt. McGuire-ID; Gant Ridge-ID; Blackbird Mtn.-ID.

If you like to fish or just want to experience a bounty of beautiful high-mountain lakes, the Crags area is well worth the trip. This trail system offers many hikes from the Crags Campground along Crags Ridge and down one of the Clear Creek–Garden Creek area trails or along Crags Ridge to Terrace Lakes and down Waterfall Creek. Other dead-end trails lead to Ship Island Lake, Buck Lake, and Puddin Lakes. Most of the trails are relatively easy with elevation grades of less than 10 percent, though a few have slightly steeper stretches. The two most distant lakes from the Crags campground are Ship Island Lake at 12 miles and Buck Lake at 13 miles. Several trails exist in the Bighorn Crags area for hiking and horseback riding, and they are all accessed by taking Trail #021 out of the campground.

There are many good campsites within the Crags, and there are a few at Birdbill, Heart, Big Clear, Airplane, Terrace, and Welcome Lake that also have primitive toilets. These sites are popular with people on horseback.

Take Trail #021 3.5 miles along a ridgeline to the junction with Trail #45. This trail travels for 2 miles before the junction with Trail #147 at Welcome Lake. The trail then continues on to its dead end at Buck Lake; the route is studded with nine other scenic lakes.

Rainbow and/or cutthroat trout exist in most of the lakes, and California golden trout are in Big Clear and Golden Trout Lakes. Bighorn sheep, mountain goat, deer, and sometimes elk and bear are seen in the area, as well as small mammals and birds. State hunting and fishing licenses are required if you intend to fish or hunt in season. A special permit is also required when hunting sheep or goat. Elk and deer are included in the general hunt.

Sawtooth Wilderness

Location: West-central Idaho, 3 miles west of Stanley.
Size: 217,000 acres; an additional 18,445 acres are proposed for wilderness designation (USDAFS).
Administration: USDAFS, Sawtooth National Recreation Area, Sawtooth National Forest.
Management status: Wilderness.
Ecosystems: Middle Rocky Mountain coniferous forest/alpine meadow province characterized by steep, glaciated overthrust mountains with sharp alpine ridges and cirques at higher elevations; western side characterized by Douglas fir and western spruce–fir forest types interspersed with meadows and perennial streams.
Elevation range: 8,797 feet at Big Buck Mountain to 10,776 feet at Thompson Peak.
System trails: 247 miles.
Maximum core to perimeter distance: 15 miles.
Activities: Camping, hiking, backpacking, fishing, photography, climbing, and cross-country skiing.
Best months: July, August, and September.
Maps: Mt. Cramer-ID; Snowyside Peak-ID; Stanley-ID; Stanley Lake-ID; Warbonnet Peak-ID; Mt. Everly-ID; Grandjean-ID; Edaho Mtn.-ID; Nahneke Mtn.-ID; Atlanta West-ID; Atlanta East-ID (USGS 1:1,000,000); 1990 Sawtooth National Recreation Area Visitor Map (includes the Sawtooth Wilderness).

OVERVIEW The Sawtooth Wilderness is a component of the 756,000-acre Sawtooth National Recreation Area (SNRA). The SNRA is part of the Sawtooth National Forest and was designated as such by Congress in 1972. The Sawtooth Wilderness is on the western edge of the SNRA complex, due west of the small town of Stanley, which serves as a staging area for visitors who wish to access the wilderness and roadless areas within short distance of the town. Due to its location (a plain) and elevation (6,200 feet), Stanley holds the distinction of being one of the coldest places in the lower forty-eight states; winter temperatures can easily drop as low as -50 degrees F.

The Sawtooth Range, which is within the wilderness, is compact and dramatic. The range is a product of the Sawtooth fault. Approximately fifty million years ago this fault forced the Sawtooth range to rise to the southwest of Stanley, while dropping the site of the future town into the Stanley Basin. Facing Stanley, peaks in the range appear to be stacked closely together and composed of various textures of pink granite. Forty of these peaks exceed 10,000 feet in elevation. Behind this impressive facade the mountains make a more gradual descent as they stretch to the west.

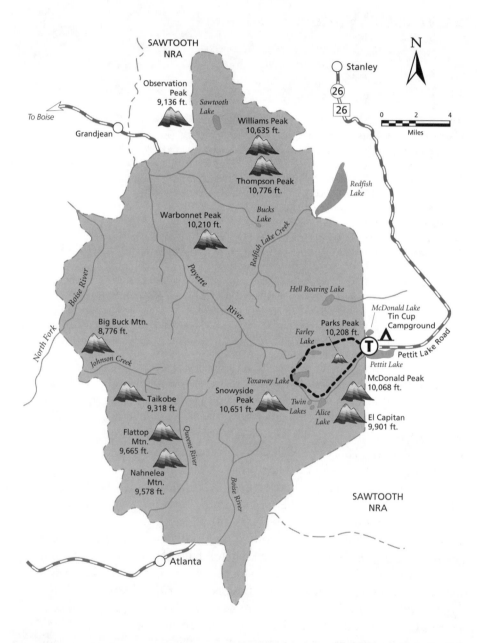

SAWTOOTH
NRA

N

Observation
Peak
9,136 ft.

*Sawtooth
Lake*

Stanley

To Boise

Grandjean

26

26

0   2   4
Miles

Williams Peak
10,635 ft.

Thompson Peak
10,776 ft.

*Redfish
Lake*

Warbonnet Peak
10,210 ft.

*Bucks
Lake*

Redfish Lake Creek

Payette

River

Hell Roaring Lake

McDonald Lake Tin Cup
Campground

Big Buck Mtn.
8,776 ft.

Boise River

North Fork

Johnson Creek

*Farley
Lake*

Parks Peak
10,208 ft.

T

Pettit Lake Road

Pettit Lake

Taikobe
9,318 ft.

Snowyside
Peak
10,651 ft.

Toxaway Lake

*Twin
Lakes*

*Alice
Lake*

McDonald Peak
10,068 ft.

El Capitan
9,901 ft.

Flattop
Mtn.
9,665 ft.

Queens River

Nahnelea
Mtn.
9,578 ft.

Boise River

SAWTOOTH
NRA

Atlanta

The upper reaches of the Sawtooth Wilderness are scattered with hundreds of tiny alpine lakes and enduring snow fields. Above the tree line the terrain features rock fields, and the lower elevations support extensive forests of spruce, fir, and ponderosa and lodgepole pine interspersed with open meadows. Farther down the slopes the forests give way to the sagebrush and short grasses that will continue down to the floor of the basin. The wilderness encompasses an area roughly 30 miles long by 18 miles wide.

The deep snows sustain the 300 cirque lakes and countless feeder streams in the Sawtooth Wilderness. These streams combine to form the headwaters of four of Idaho's major rivers: the Payette, Big Wood, Salmon, and Boise.

Big-game species are not common due to the deep snow, rugged terrain, and extreme temperatures, but the windswept high country is home to one of Idaho's largest populations of mountain goats. Redfish Lake, on the northeastern border of the wilderness, received its name from the spawning ground of sockeye salmon, which turn a deep red during the spawning season. A number of salmon make it back to this clear lake each year to spawn.

RECREATIONAL USES The entire complex is readily accessible by good trails and major roads and so enjoys extensive use from visitors in the summer months. The portion of the Sawtooth National Recreation Area that lies east of Stanley and encompasses the White Cloud and Boulder Mountains (162,740 acres proposed for wilderness designation) takes the brunt of this traffic as sections of it are open to snowmobile traffic and motorbike use.

Summer activities such as hiking and horseback riding are popular in the rugged Sawtooth Wilderness; trails are well maintained. The tall and jagged faces of the Sawtooths also provide a wide range of rock-climbing opportunities, ranging from free climbs to advanced technical climbs.

Due to the deep snow and ruggedness of the eastern side, cross-country skiing is limited to the fringes of the wilderness; however, cross-country skiing can be enjoyed if you launch from the west, such as from the towns of Grandjean and Atlanta. Likewise, the eastern side of Sawtooth is not as accessible for casual, easy hikes, but the western side opens up and trails are not excessively steep. All of the trails within the wilderness follow the general course of the numerous creeks as they flow out of the mountains.

Many of the backcountry lakes—most with fish—can be found alongside trails. At lower elevations lakes are stocked with fish; native trout, including rainbow, cutthroat, brown, golden, and brook, are found at higher elevations.

New wilderness regulations are in effect specifying that permits are required for horses, that all dogs must be on a leash, and that fires are to be contained in a portable, self-contained fire box. Check with the Forest Service in Stanley for specific regulations.

Stanley Lake lies at the northeastern corner of the jagged Sawtooth Range.

HOW TO GET THERE *Pettit–Toxaway Loop:* From Stanley drive 13.5 miles south on Idaho Highway 75 to mile post 170.3 and the Pettit Lake Road turnoff. Continue 1.6 miles to a four-way junction and turn right to the Tin Cup trailhead.

Day Hike or Overnighter

Pettit–Toxaway Loop

Distance: 17-mile loop.
Difficulty: Moderately strenuous.
Topo map: Snowside Peak-ID.

Exceptional views of the Sawtooth Range and priceless fishing make this a great introduction to the Sawtooth Wilderness. This hike begins at Tin Cup Campground at Pettit Lake; the lake itself is quite beautiful and offers exceptional fishing for a variety of trout species. The entire hike will feature an elevation gain of approximately 2,500 feet.

To get to Alice Lake follow the left-hand branch of the trail as it follows the shoreline. You will be heading upstream and following the creek drainage past McDonald Peak on the left. Alice Lake will be the first lake you come to, with El Capitan Peak rising dramatically behind it. The trail continues on to Twin Lakes on the left. Alice and Twin Lakes contain stocked brook trout. It is a fairly easy additional 2 miles to Toxaway Lake. Toxaway Lake is the biggest lake of this bunch, and there are several good campsites here. Like the lakes preceding it, Toxaway is an angler's dream, with numerous brook trout within. From Toxaway Lake the trail heads downstream, with one creek crossing and views of waterfalls. From Toxaway Lake it is approximately 4 miles to Farley Lake and another 4 miles back to the trailhead at Pettit Lake.

Selway–Bitterroot Wilderness   13

Location: North-central Idaho and western Montana, 50 miles southwest of Missoula, Montana.
Size: 1,239,840 acres; an additional 24,500 acres are proposed for wilderness designation (USDAFS).
Administration: USDAFS, Bitterroot, Lolo, Clearwater, and Nez Perce National Forests.
Management status: Wilderness.
Ecosystems: Middle Rocky Mountain coniferous forest/alpine meadow province, Idaho Batholith section, characterized by strongly glaciated mountains with cirques and large U-shaped valleys; Lower Tertiary and Mesozoic granite; grand fir–Douglas fir, western spruce-fir, and western ponderosa forest types; many perennial streams and high-elevation lakes.
Elevation range: 1,800 feet on the Selway River to 8,817 feet at Ranger Peak.
System trails: 600 miles.
Maximum core to perimeter distance: 25 miles.
Activities: Hiking, backpacking, horseback riding, cross-country skiing, rafting, kayaking, and fishing.
Best months: June, July, and August.
Maps: Ranger Peak-ID; Savage Ridge-ID; White Sand Lake-ID; Huckleberry Butte-ID; Greenside Butte-ID; Fish Lake-ID; McConnell Mtn.-ID; Hungry Rock-ID; Cedar Ridge-ID; Jeanette Mtn.-ID; Blodgett Mtn.-ID; Chimney Peak-ID; Fenn Mtn.-ID; Big Rock Mtn.-ID; Shissler Peak-ID; Freeman Peak-ID; Wahoo Peak-ID; Saddle Mtn.-ID; Tenmile Lake-ID; Selway Falls-ID; Fog Mtn.-ID; Mink Peak-ID; Moose Ridge-ID; Dog Creek-ID; Twin Butte-ID; Hunter Peak-ID; El Capitan-ID; Anderson Butte-ID; Vermillion Peak-ID; Running Lake-ID; Wylies Peak-ID; Gardiner Peak-ID; Mt. George-ID; Mt. Paloma-ID; Tin Cup Lake-ID; Sable Hill-ID; Green Mtn.-ID; Three Prong Mtn.-ID; Spot Mtn.-ID; Burnt Strip Mtn.-ID; Watchtower Peak-ID; Boston Mtn.-ID; Spread Creek Point-ID; Sabe Mtn.-ID; Magruder Mtn.-ID; Beaver Jack Mtn.-ID; Nez Perce Peak-ID; Sheep Hill-ID; Dennis Mtn.-ID; Stripe Mtn.-ID; Wood Hump-ID; Blue Joint-ID (USGS 1:1,000,000).

OVERVIEW The Selway–Bitterroot Wilderness lies in the Clearwater, Lolo, Nez Perce, and Bitterroot National Forests and was one of the first areas to be designated as wilderness under the Wilderness Act of 1964. This area encompasses more than 1.2 million acres and is part of the vast wilderness complex that lies at the heart of Idaho. The Selway–Bitterroot lies just to the north of the 2.3-million-acre Frank Church–River of No Return Wilderness Area and extends across the Bitterroot Divide into Montana. The Magruder Corridor, a dirt road that connects Elk City, Idaho, to Darby, Montana, is the dividing line between the two wilderness areas.

13A SELWAY–BITTERROOT WILDERNESS (OVERVIEW)

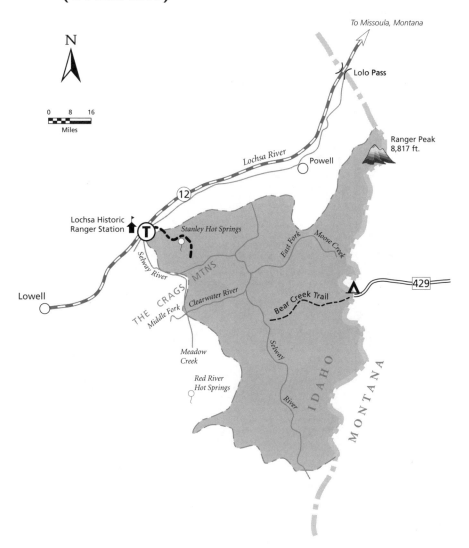

Like its cousin to the south, the Selway–Bitterroot is a land of dense forests and steep mountains cut with canyons carved by multiple rivers. Numerous high-country lakes feed these rivers, and marshes are notable at lower elevations. Near the rivers the forests give way to thick brush that includes the huckleberry. What is most notable in this wilderness are the rivers. The Selway–Bitterroot is home to the Middle Fork of the Clearwater, which includes the Lochsa and

13B   SELWAY–BITTERROOT WILDERNESS (STANLEY HOT SPRINGS AND SELWAY CRAGS)

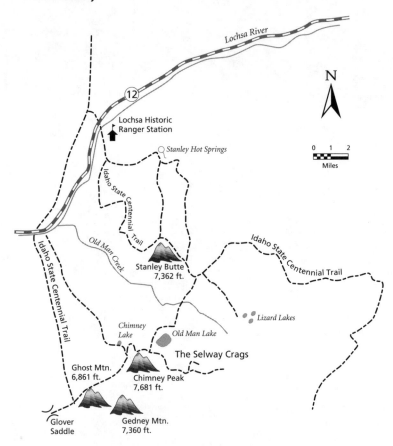

Selway. These rivers are not only famous for their white water, they are also reasonably approachable, with many good access roads.

The area lies in a portion of what once was the homeland of the Nez Perce. The northern portion of the wilderness is bordered by the Lochsa River, which means "rough water" in the Nez Perce tongue. Idaho Highway 12 follows this river, as did the Lewis and Clark expedition in 1805. There is a very steep and rugged road, the Lolo Motorway, that more closely approximates their journey; the Lolo Trail does likewise. (See the Introduction for more information about the Nez Perce and Lewis and Clark.) The wilderness was named for the Selway and Bitterroot Rivers that flow through its expanse. The Bitterroot River was named after a staple in the Nez Perce diet, the root of the Bitterroot plant.

Big game animals reside within these borders, including elk, mule and white-tailed deer, grizzly and black bear, and mountain lion. The many clear streams and high-mountain lakes provide prime habitat for several species of trout. All of these animals are largely undisturbed as the wilderness is extremely rugged and remote, and passage is accomplished only by horseback, foot, or boat.

RECREATIONAL USES The Selway–Bitterroot Wilderness is a great destination for hikers because of the many available trails. Numerous trails follow or intersect with the rivers for some outstanding day hikes. The trails can be extended east into Montana and south into the Frank Church for an unparalleled backcountry experience.

The Lochsa and Selway Rivers receive the most use as a number of people have discovered the challenging technical rapids that draw kayakers and rafters from around the world. The Lochsa begins in the Bitterroot Mountains of Montana and eventually joins the Selway and Clearwater Rivers. What attracts white-water enthusiasts, beside the wilderness experience, is the more than forty Class III–IV rapids. The Lochsa River parallels Idaho Highway 12 on its long and winding path from Lolo Pass on the Idaho–Montana border into Lowell, Idaho. For the most part the highway is visible from the river and detracts somewhat from the experience; however, there is not substantial traffic on this route as there are no towns along it and the drive from Lolo Pass to Lowell takes more than four hours. The Selway River offers a more secluded white-water and wilderness experience. The Forest Service encourages this by limiting boat launches along the river's 60 miles. The Selway offers plenty of rafting challenge as the rapids are numerous, and during the spring runoff they reach Class IV–V intensity.

There are plenty of rainbow and bull trout, native westslope cutthroat trout, whitefish, and steelhead in the rivers in the spring. Check with the Idaho Department of Fish and Game for current regulations.

Hunting for big-game species is a popular fall pastime in the wilderness, but there's also an abundance of upland bird species such as turkey, pheasant, and several types of grouse.

HOW TO GET THERE *Stanley Hot Springs:* From Lowell follow Idaho Highway 12 along the Lochsa River approximately 22 miles to the Lochsa Historic Ranger Station on the left. This is worth a stop as there are log buildings here preserved from the 1920s. About 0.5 mile farther up the road there is a campground and access to the trailhead.

Selway Crags: See narrative under "Selway Crags."

Day Hike

Stanley Hot Springs

Distance: 6 miles round-trip.
Difficulty: Easy.
Topo map: Huckleberry Butte, ID.

This is an easy hike to some great hot springs. From the campground and trail-head the trail will follow Boulder Creek upstream approximately 3 miles to the springs. There is no huge elevation gain, just a nice walk with a little hike at the end to the springs themselves. This trip is great as an end unto itself but may be combined with the next hike.

Day Hike or Overnighter

Selway Crags

Distance: 24 miles round-trip.
Difficulty: Moderately strenuous.
Topo maps: Chimney Peak-ID; Huckleberry Butte-ID; Fenn Mtn.-ID; Greenside Butte-ID.

The Crags are noted for their sheer beauty as well as for the numerous tiny lakes lying amongst them. The spectacular Chimney Peak adds to the view on the west. Great views and solitude are augmented by exceptional fishing opportunities at Chimney Lake and Old Man Lake.

From Stanley Hot Springs the trail splits in two. Take the left-hand trail for an easier route. Both trails end up connecting at the Idaho Centennial Trail. From here the trail heads southeast around Stanley Butte before dropping down into the drainage of Old Man Creek. Follow the creek upstream to Old Man Lake and then into the Crags on the east. There are many good campsites here from which you can further explore the area.

Hell's Canyon Wilderness Area

14

Location: West-central Idaho and northeastern Oregon, 8 miles west of Riggins, Idaho.
Size: Approximately 84,800 acres in Idaho (127,000 acres in Oregon).
Administration: BLM.
Management status: Wilderness.
Ecosystems: Great Plains/Palouse dry steppe province characterized by semi-arid, rolling plateaus cut by deep river canyons and dominated by extensive grasslands; this steppe is comprised of short grasses usually bunched and sparsely distributed, allowing for much soil exposure.
Elevation range: 1,480 feet at Snake River to 8,492 feet at White Mountain.
System trails: 900 miles within the entire Hell's Canyon National Recreation Area (NRA).
Maximum core to perimeter distance: 5.5 miles.
Activities: Fishing, hiking, rafting, and horseback riding.
Best months: May, June, and July.
Maps: Kirkwood Creek-ID/OR; Lucile-ID; Old Timer Mtn.-ID/OR; Kessler Creek-ID; Squirrel Prairie-ID/OR; He Devil-ID; Heavens Gate-ID; White Monument-ID/OR; Purgatory Saddle-ID (USGS 1:1,000,000).

OVERVIEW The Hell's Canyon National Recreation Area was created on December 31, 1975, as the result of the work of Senator Frank Church. Local power companies were proposing to dam the Snake River, but Church fought hard to halt the process. Creation of the Hell's Canyon National Recreation Area, sponsored by Senator Church, staved off the power companies and protected the area from any further construction plans. Its creation also served to protect the area's archaeological and historical attributes. The Hell's Canyon National Recreation Area includes the Hell's Canyon Wilderness Area, which includes the Snake River. The Snake River, which passes through and created Hell's Canyon, is the border between western Idaho and eastern Oregon. The greater NRA allows for all varieties of off-road use, whereas the wilderness bans the use of all motorized vehicles.

The canyon was created by normal stream erosion as the Snake River cut a path through soft rock. This erosion was accelerated by melting glaciers as well as by the spillover of Lake Bonneville, the prehistoric lake that covered a large portion of Idaho and northern Utah at one time. These two events caused increased volumes of water to flow downstream through Hell's Canyon. This huge flow of water sharply increased the width and depth of the canyon and created several terraces within it.

14A HELL'S CANYON WILDERNESS AREA (OVERVIEW)

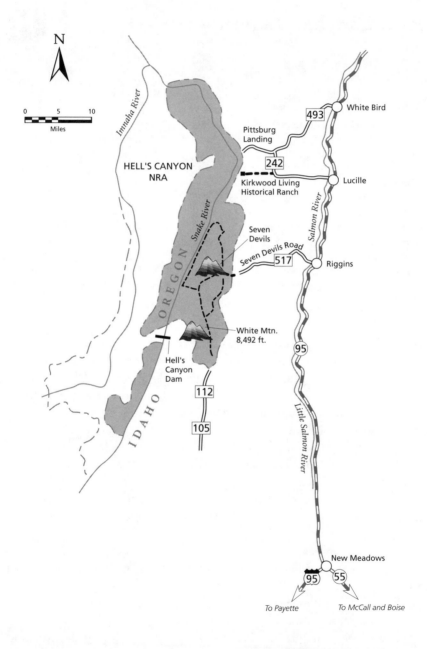

14B HELL'S CANYON WILDERNESS AREA (SEVEN DEVILS)

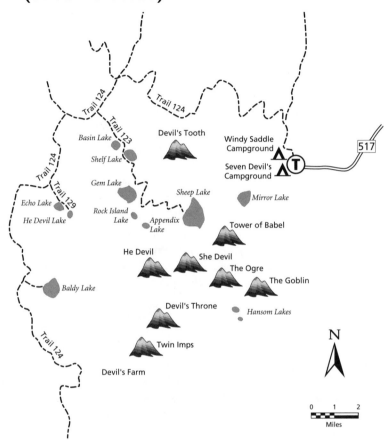

The lower reaches of the canyon, along the river, support desert plants such as sagebrush and cactus that thrive on arid conditions. The streams that feed into the Snake are lined with deciduous bushes and trees. These give way to spruce and fir as the landscape heads up into the mountains above the canyon. These mountains support Engelmann spruce and subalpine fir.

Due to the variations in habitat, many types of animal species either live here year-round or use the area on their migration route. Black bear, cougar, elk, deer, mountain goat, pronghorn antelope, and bighorn sheep are plentiful at the higher, forested elevations. At lower elevations along the river, desert animals such as the rattlesnake can be found. The Snake River is part of the migration route of the sockeye salmon as it travels from the Pacific Ocean to its spawning grounds in Redfish Lake at the base of the Sawtooth Mountains near Stanley. (See chapter 12, the Sawtooth Wilderness, for more information.)

The human history of the canyon is long and varied. Some Nez Perce have made this canyon their home for more than 7,000 years. Artifacts have been discovered at thousands of sites throughout the area. These include petroglyphs, pictographs, pit houses, and tool making sites. Due to a treaty dispute, the Nez Perce were displaced at one time to reservations in Washington State and Oklahoma. Today they have regained some of their traditional lands in what is now the Nez Perce Indian Reservation, just east of the river. They retain hunting and fishing rights within the Hell's Canyon National Recreation Area. (See the Introduction for more information.)

Evidence of other inhabitants also abounds. Abandoned homesteader cabins, mines, and the Kirkwood Living Historical Ranch are located along the canyon's floor. The Kirkwood Living Historical Ranch is an interpretive center located on the Idaho side of the Snake River, 5 miles upriver by trail or water from Pittsburg Landing. The ranch features a museum and historical buildings from the 1800s; it was the home of former Idaho senator and governor Len Jordan, who lived there with his family during the Depression. Access to the ranch is via Forest Road 493, Deer Creek Road. (The turnoff from Idaho Highway 95 is just south of White Bird.) Travel 10 miles from Forest Road 493 to Pittsburg Saddle and another 7 miles to the lower Pittsburg Landing.

RECREATIONAL USES The Hell's Canyon NRA and Wilderness is a huge land area administered by two states, Idaho and Oregon, and split by the Snake River. As such, it struggles to fulfill many visions and goals within its borders.

The importance of preserving the free-flowing character of the Snake River was the impetus for designating 67 miles of the river as a Wild and Scenic river. This protected the canyon from any future threat of dams and also ensured the survival of several rare and endangered fish species that use the river as a crucial migration route, including Chinook and Sockeye salmon, as well as redband trout and prehistoric white sturgeon. (See chapter 1, Long Canyon, for more information on the white sturgeon.) These species are protected, but anglers may be allowed to use catch-and-release techniques; check current regulations with the Idaho Department of Fish and Game.

Fishing, boating, rafting, and camping on the banks of the Snake River are great ways to experience the drama of the canyon and view the wildlife.

The sections of the Snake River that are not protected by wilderness designation offer completely different experiences. On these stretches jet boats are not only allowed, they are loud and numerous as many companies conduct river excursions. The trails above the river are also busy places as dirt bikes are in use in the summer and snowmachines in the winter. However, the Forest Service is considering placing tighter restrictions on recreational activities in the canyon. Its new proposal would close approximately 76 percent of the

Gateway to Hell's Canyon, the Salmon River at Riggins is a popular launching point for rafters.

roads in the Hell's Canyon National Recreation Area and reduce motor boat use. Conservation groups are pushing for the creation of a Hell's Canyon/Chief Joseph National Park and Preserve in order to better protect and preserve this area from the impact of motor boats and other motorized traffic. The proposal is still under consideration by the BLM, but there is vigorous opposition being voiced by outfitters and recreationists.

Due to the rich and varied human history in this area, archaeological exploration and study are important and diverse as researchers scrutinize the thousands of identified sites in and around Hell's Canyon. The Hell's Canyon region has been in continuous human use for an estimated 7,000 years, from early Native Americans to Chinese miners to modern-day ranchers. The Forest Service has restored several old structures; well-maintained trails lead to these. Beside the officially identified sites, backcountry travel can uncover other evidence of former inhabitants. These artifacts are protected by law and must be left undisturbed, but the prospect of discovery adds spice to the surrounding natural beauty.

HOW TO GET THERE *Seven Devils:* From Boise take Idaho Highway 55 north. At New Meadows go north on U.S. Highway 95. Just south of the town of Riggins turn left onto Forest Road 517. There are two campgrounds at the terminus of Forest Road 517; the Seven Devils trail starts from the Windy Saddle Campground.

Snake River Trail: Access is at Pittsburg Landing, which is 17 miles from U.S. 95, southwest of White Bird, Idaho, on Forest Road 493.

Overnight Hike

Seven Devils

Distance: 27 miles round-trip.
Difficulty: Moderately strenuous.
Topo map: He Devil-ID.

This hike accentuates some of the best of the Hell's Canyon Wilderness. Awe-inspiring views and the opportunity for rock climbing and/or fishing high-mountain lakes make for a valuable experience.

The Seven Devils range divides Hell's Canyon and the Salmon River Canyon and is accessed at the Windy Saddle trailhead (Seven Devils).

This trail travels around the peaks of the Seven Devils Mountains; a good campsite can be made at Sheep Lake for an overnighter. The lake is approximately 8 miles from the trailhead.

The trail is relatively easy with some switchbacks and mild elevation gains. You will travel through meadows and alongside several small ponds and a few good-size lakes that contain a number of fish. The trail travels around Devil's Tooth and then down into a basin that contains Sheep Lake. Sheep Lake itself is encircled by the spires of the Seven Devils, including He and She Devils and the Tower of Babel, which rises more than 1,000 feet from the banks of the lake. Good trails abound here for exploring the peaks.

Extended Overnight Hike

Snake River Trail

Distance: 29 miles one way.
Difficulty: Strenuous.
Topo maps: Kirkwood Creek-ID/OR; Temperence Creek-ID/OR; Old Timer Mtn.-ID/OR; Squirrel Prairie-ID/OR; White Monument-ID/OR.

This trail highlights the unique geological features of the canyon. The oldest rocks here belong to old volcanic islands, part of ancient Lake Bonneville, which once covered large portions of Idaho and northern Utah. These rocks display this history by their steeply tilted layers. Basalt forms the bulk of the canyon walls and the tall gravel bars are reminders of the Lake Bonneville spillover. Fishing is great in here, as is camping along the banks of the river.

This trail parallels the Snake River and is an out-and-back hike as there is no loop option. It exits at Hell's Canyon Dam.

The trip is recommended for summer or fall. Due to the run off from melting snows upstream (above 40,000 cubic feet per second), portions of the trail may be underwater when the river is running high in the spring.

Boulder/White Cloud Mountains   15

Location: Central Idaho, 8 miles north of Ketchum.
Size: 190,350 acres (Sawtooth National Forest) and 40,020 acres (Challis National Forest).
Administration: USDAFS, Sawtooth and Challis National Forests.
Management status: Proposed wilderness.
Ecosystems: Middle Rocky Mountain steppe/coniferous forest/alpine meadow province characterized by complex and high, steep mountains with sharp ridges and cirques; Precambrian granite, sedimentary and volcanic rocks; Douglas fir forest type with sagebrush steppe and smaller areas of alpine vegetation.
Elevation range: 9,376 feet at Potoman Peak to 11,815 feet at Castle Peak.
System trails: 280 miles.
Maximum core to perimeter distance: 20 miles.
Activities: Backpacking, fishing, hunting, horseback riding, skiing, climbing, and cross-country skiing.
Best months: June, July, and August.
Maps: Stanley-ID; Casino Bar-ID; Robinson Bar-ID; Livingston Creek-ID; Potaman Creek-ID; Obsidian-ID; Washington Peak-ID; Boulder Chain Lakes-ID; Bowery Creek-ID; Alturas Lake-ID; Horton Peak-ID; Galena Peak-ID; Ryan Peak-ID; Galena-ID; Easley Hot Springs-ID; Amber Lakes-ID (USGS 1:1,000,000).

OVERVIEW The Boulder/White Cloud Mountains are the range of peaks and canyons that form the eastern edge of the narrow Sawtooth Valley. The northernmost mountains are referred to as the White Clouds and the southern ones as the Boulders. Their northern border is formed by the East Fork of the Salmon River, and they extend southeast from there, dropping off into the town of Ketchum. Due to the unique roadless character through most of its expanse, the area is currently under consideration for a wilderness designation by the Forest Service. In the meantime it is classified as a proposed wilderness.

The Boulder/White Cloud Mountains are a part of the greater Sawtooth National Recreation Area (SNRA) that also includes the Sawtooth Wilderness and the Sawtooth Valley, with the town of Stanley lying in its center. The SNRA is part of the Sawtooth National Forest and was designated as such by Congress in 1972.

The White Clouds are formed primarily of white limestone and this feature has given them their name; the Boulders are also aptly named. The combined ranges are prime habitat for large herds of elk, deer, and antelope and serve as migration routes and winter range for these big-game animals.

15   BOULDER/WHITE CLOUD MOUNTAINS

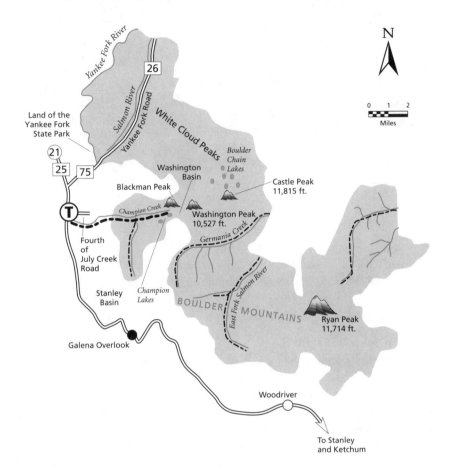

All of the land in and around the Stanley Basin appears dry and with minimal vegetation. However, numerous streams, springs, and lakes originate in these mountains and contribute their waters to four of Idaho's major rivers: the Payette, Big Wood, Salmon, and Boise. The land is federally unprotected but is essentially wilderness in its character, as most visitors explore only the range's fringes, and hikers and climbers tend to seek out the more dramatic looking Sawtooth Mountains to the west. In fact the area is so overlooked that most of the peaks in this system have never even been named; instead, they've been given the initials WCP (White Cloud Peak) and a number.

The trails that do exist are largely due to the area's old ties to mining activity. Mining is no longer allowed, but evidence of the past abounds. Old mines, equipment, and cabins can be found throughout the range, and most of the

The Boulder Mountains form the northern backdrop for the towns of Ketchum and Sun Valley.

access roads are still passable (though not maintained and treacherous at times). The buildings are also not maintained and so are deteriorating. Use care when exploring near old mine sites as these buildings could collapse, and the mines themselves are not marked and are completely unsafe.

RECREATIONAL USES Maybe it's because of their more dramatic cousins to the west, but the Boulder/White Cloud Mountains have seen a different type of recreational activity than the Sawtooth Range. In fact little of this area has even been named let alone maintained. Due to this fact, hikers and climbers have migrated to the Sawtooths while abandoning the Boulder/White Clouds to the people who seek a different type of experience.

Snowmachine and dirt bike usage is allowed but is primarily engaged in the foothills of these mountains; a true wilderness experience *is* definitely possible in the Boulder/White Cloud backcountry.

Fishing is paramount in the Sawtooth Valley and the SNRA; the sportfishing industry is thriving here, with anglers seeking the abundant trout, steelhead, and salmon. The crystal clear, cold water provides excellent habitat for these fish and also furnishes them with critical spawning grounds. There are also numerous hot springs. Several good trails lead to these sites.

If cultural history is of interest to you, ample evidence abounds. After the initial gold prospecting, miners sought out other minerals, and mining was a big industry here in the 1930s and 40s. There are still plenty of standing miners' cabins, mining sites, and mining artifacts scattered throughout the area. More mining history can be explored by entering Stanley and the SNRA from the north on Yankee Fork Road. Here you will find the Land of the Yankee Fork Idaho State Park. There's a ghost town of the gold rush era of the 1870s as well as maintained evidence of the methods that kept this site actively mined well into the 1950s.

HOW TO GET THERE *Washington Peak:* From Stanley take Idaho Highway 75 south 16 miles to the Fourth of July Creek Road (it's 1 mile past the Sawtooth Valley interpretive sign). Drive 1 mile on this road and take the right-hand road at the Y. Proceed another 1.5 miles to the trailhead.

Day Hike

Washington Peak

Distance: 7 miles one way.
Difficulty: Easy.
Topo maps: Obsidian-ID; Washington Peak-ID.

This is a great archaeological hike, as evidence of old mining activity abounds, and there are numerous abandoned cabins here.

The trail follows Champion Creek and skirts the Champion Lakes, heading south and then east to the abandoned mining sites. A primitive road leads into this area from the other side (east), so be prepared for company from this point.

Once at the site you will want to explore the roughly 2-mile-square area that includes Washington Basin, Washington Creek, Washington Peak (10,527 feet), and Blackman Peak, all named after a black miner, George Washington Blackman, who pioneered mining in the area in 1875. Cabins, mines, and mining equipment are interspersed throughout the area, and artifacts are easy to find (though by law and by honor, they must remain where found).

Gospel Hump Wilderness   16

Location: Central Idaho, 32 miles southeast of Grangeville.
Size: 200,464 acres.
Administration: USDAFS, Nez Perce National Forest.
Management status: Wilderness.
Ecosystems: Middle Rocky Mountain coniferous forest/alpine meadow province, Idaho Batholith section, characterized by strongly glaciated mountains with cirques and U-shaped valleys; Douglas fir, western spruce-fir, and western ponderosa forest types with many perennial streams and high-elevation lakes.
Elevation range: 1,920 feet at Wind River Bridge to 8,938 feet at Buffalo Hump.
System trails: 260 miles.
Maximum core to perimeter distance: 11 miles.
Activities: Backpacking, camping, hiking, and horseback riding.
Best months: June, July, and August.
Maps: Sawyer Ridge-ID; Sourdough Peak-ID; North Pole-ID; Hanover Mtn.-ID; Marble Butte-ID; Buffalo Hump-ID; Carey Dome-ID; Johnson Butte-ID; Cottontail Point-ID; Florence, Dairy Mtn.-ID; Orogrande-ID; Columbia Ridge-ID; Silverspur Ridge-ID; Mackay Bar-ID (USGS 1:1,000,000).

OVERVIEW The Gospel Hump Wilderness, formed under the Central Idaho Wilderness Act of 1980, adjoins the Frank Church–River of No Return Wilderness Area to the southeast. On a map the area appears as a large thumb-like protrusion from the great Frank Church, and it contains many of the same ecological characteristics as the Frank Church. (See chapter 11, Frank Church–River of No Return Wilderness Area, for more information.)

The Gospel Hump Wilderness is an area of moderate-size mountains that are thickly wooded. The highest point in the wilderness is Buffalo Hump at an elevation of only 8,938 feet. The distinctive feature of the Gospel Hump is its comprehensive network of creeks and streams. These waters provide habitat and spawning grounds for numerous native fish, including bull, rainbow, and cutthroat trout and Chinook salmon. In the southern half of the wilderness, the streams all flow toward and into the Main Salmon River. The Sheep Creek drainage is the most impressive of these. The creek originates in Buffalo Hump, and through the centuries it has carved a sheer canyon before emptying into the Salmon River.

16   GOSPEL HUMP WILDERNESS

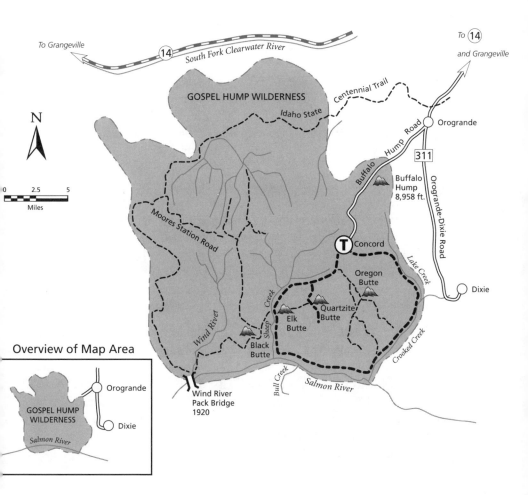

The northern expanse of the wilderness contains somewhat tamer terrain, and the lakes and streams located here all flow north into the South Fork of the Clearwater River. Due to the terrain and closer access roads, these northern waters provide easier fishing.

The entire area receives abundant rainfall, and the underbrush is very thick. Stands of Douglas fir, ponderosa and lodgepole pine, Engelmann spruce, western larch, and western cedar grow quite densely in this region. The thick vegetation provides excellent habitat for black bear, white-tailed and mule deer, moose, and grizzlies transplanted from British Columbia.

RECREATIONAL USES The Gospel Hump Wilderness is a true wilderness; most of the trails experience minimal use, and only about half of them receive regular maintenance. Hiking is therefore a challenging, as well as a rewarding, experience. The trailheads can be crowded during the peak summer and fall seasons, but hike 10 miles into the interior and you will find a true, back-country wilderness adventure.

The Sheep Creek drainage is an excellent destination, and there is a good trail that starts at Concord and follows Sheep Creek to the Salmon River. Two Forest Service lookouts, one located at Black Butte on the west side and the other at Quartzite Butte on the east, would also be great destinations for the impressive views they provide of Sheep Creek canyon and the surrounding wilderness.

Beside hiking, hunting is the most popular fall pastime here, as the thick underbrush provides excellent forage and cover for all species of big-game animals. Several outfitters provide hunts into the wilderness; hunting is limited to horseback and on foot so the impact is minimal. Thus, backcountry experiences are noted for their solitude even in the fall. Check with the Idaho Department of Fish and Game for current season dates to either target or avoid them.

Fishing is exceptional in the Gospel Hump wilderness, and the lakes and streams due north of the Moores Station Road provide the easiest access.

HOW TO GET THERE *Elk Butte:* From Orogrande travel south on Buffalo Hump Road for 11 miles to Concord. The Elk Butte trailhead is located here.

Sheep Creek: From Grangeville take Idaho Highway 13 east 8 miles to the junction with Idaho Highway 14. Take ID 14 south. Drive approximately 40 miles to Crooked Creek Road and turn right. The town of Orogrande is 9 miles farther. From there you take Buffalo Hump Road south 12 miles to Concord and the trailhead. Buffalo Hump, the highest point in the wilderness, will be visible along the road to the west.

Day Hike

Elk Butte

Distance: 15 miles round-trip.
Difficulty: Easy to moderate.
Topo map: Marble Butte-ID.

This is a fairly easy hike, with the opportunity to experience some of the high-mountain lakes in the region. It also provides for a good jumping-off point for additional hikes.

From the Elk Butte trailhead, the hike proceeds along the East Fork of Sheep Creek for 5 miles to the Elk Butte Trail. This trail goes due south for 2 miles where it will split. You can continue south the short distance to the Quartzite Butte, which lies to the east, and Black Butte to the south. Both of these have Forest Service lookout towers. Elk Butte is west another 2.5 miles on the trail over Green Saddle.

Additional hikes accessed from this trail include Slate Lake and Moores Lake, Beargrass Ridge, Plummer Mountain, and Hanover.

Extended Overnight Hike

Sheep Creek

Distance: 38 miles round-trip.
Difficulty: Moderately difficult.
Topo maps: Buffalo Hump-ID; Silverspur Ridge-ID; Cottontail Point-ID.

This hike offers the opportunity to experience the most dramatic feature in the Gospel Hump, the Sheep Creek canyon. The trail also follows the Salmon River with a good campsite along its banks.

The trail leaves Concord and climbs for the first 3 miles. The trail then drops down and follows Sheep Creek for 10 miles to its rendezvous with the Salmon River. Here the trail turns east and follows the Salmon for 7 miles. This section of the river has been designated as Wild and Scenic and is still within the Buffalo Hump Wilderness boundary. There are several campsites along the river with a good one at Bull Creek, where it joins the Salmon.

At Crooked Creek the trail turns northeast and follows the creek upstream for 7 miles. The trail will continue 5 miles west to Lake Creek and a fork. Follow the left-hand trail 6 miles back to the Concord trailhead.

Meadow Creek   17

Location: North-central Idaho, 10 miles northeast of Elk City.
Size: 206,254 acres.
Administration: USDAFS, Nez Perce National Forest.
Management status: Primarily roadless, nonwilderness.
Ecosystems: Middle Rocky Mountain coniferous forest/alpine meadow province, Idaho Batholith section, characterized by strongly glaciated mountains with cirques and large U-shaped valleys; Lower Tertiary and mesozoic granite; grand fir–Douglas fir, western red cedar, western spruce-fir, and western ponderosa forest types; many perennial streams and high-elevation lakes.
Elevation range: 1,734 feet at Meadow Creek to 7,232 feet at Granite Peak.
System trails: 84 miles.
Maximum core to perimeter distance: 10 miles.
Activities: Hiking, backpacking, kayaking, fishing, and hunting.
Best months: May, June, and July.
Maps: Selway Falls-ID; Fog Mtn.-ID; Anderson Butte-ID; Vermillion Peak-ID; Blackhawk-ID; Sable Hill-ID; Running Lake-ID; Grouse Creek-ID (USGS 1:1,000,000).

OVERVIEW The Meadow Creek drainage is an extension of the Selway–Bitterroot Wilderness's west side. Meadow Creek begins within the Clearwater Mountains just north of Magruder Corridor Road. It extends north past Granite Peak and then turns sharply west into an ever-deepening canyon before heading back north again to the confluence of the Selway River and the Middle Fork of the Clearwater River. Both of these rivers offer exceptional rafting and kayaking experiences and are listed as Wild and Scenic rivers; Meadow Creek is under consideration for that same status. The last 13 miles of Meadow Creek flow through a very deep canyon that creates additional kayaking opportunities. The Idaho State Centennial Trail follows Meadow Creek through this section.

The Meadow Creek area is not being considered for wilderness designation at this time although many conservation groups continue to lobby for its inclusion in the greater Selway–Bitterroot complex. Due to its lack of protection and its proximity to access roads, the western portion of the Meadow Creek area has been logged in some sections. The eastern portion has remained wild since it is essentially contiguous with the Selway–Bitterroot.

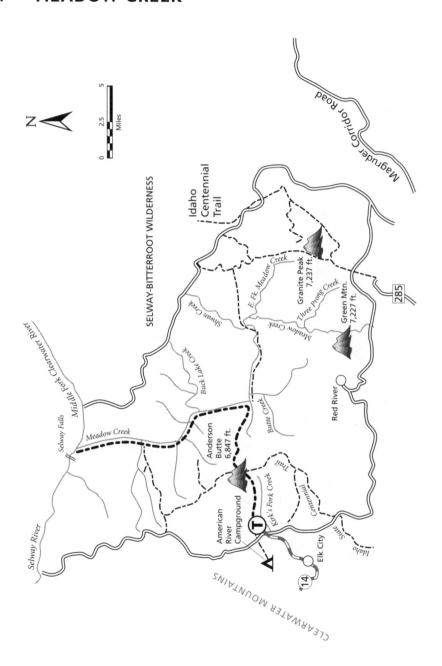

The Meadow Creek area—not notably mountainous—is characterized by heavily forested mountains and high ridges that drop off into deep canyons. These canyons contain some of Idaho's truly wild rivers, with Meadow Creek being the crown jewel. Meadow Creek is one of the largest streams in the Selway River system and also provides valuable habitat for resident cutthroat and rainbow trout, as well as spawning grounds for salmon and steelhead.

RECREATIONAL USES The dense underbrush in this area provides forage and cover for huge herds of elk, with a particularly large percentage of mature bulls, making the Meadow Creek area a mecca for big-game hunters in the fall. Ten months of the year, Elk City is a veritable ghost town, with a resident population of approximately 600. But every fall its population booms as hunters and guides move in and use this town as a jumping-off point to the backcountry. Due to this popularity prime wilderness hiking opportunities are more readily available earlier in the summer season. The trail system is not well developed and receives only moderate usage outside of the hunting season.

Beside the large number of elk, there are also populations of black bear, mountain goat, white-tailed and mule deer, moose, and mountain lion in the Meadow Creek area. Smaller species such as grouse, rabbit, and fox also enjoy the amenities provided by the thick vegetation.

Fishing Idaho's native trout species is popular in this area and well worth the hike. Meadow Creek proper has not been rated for white-water classification, but it is known as a great kayak experience for the individual willing to portage upstream for the opportunity.

Four maintained campgrounds are located at the confluence of the Selway, Middle Fork of the Clearwater, and Meadow Creek.

HOW TO GET THERE *Anderson Butte National Recreational Trail:* From Elk City take American River Road north 1 mile to American River Campground. The trailhead originates here. Trail 832 follows the American River for 5 miles before heading due east for 3 miles to Anderson Butte.

Extended Hike

Anderson Butte National Recreational Trail to Selway Falls

Distance: 20 miles one way.
Difficulty: Moderately strenuous.
Topo maps: Selway Falls-ID; Anderson Butte-ID; Blackhawk-ID; Vermillion Peak-ID.

Spectacular views, white water, steep canyons, and waterfalls describe this hike. There is no better way to get a taste of this unique area than to explore

Meadow Creek. If you're up for a serious portage, Meadow Creek can be kayaked to where it joins the Selway River.

The Anderson Butte National Recreational Trail starts off by skirting Kirk's Fork Creek for 5 miles to Anderson Butte. There is a lookout tower here with a great view. The trail here has joined the Idaho Centennial Trail, and you will continue on this as you turn right at the tower. The trail will follow the ridge-line for approximately 4 miles, at which point it will drop down to Butte Creek. This is the headwaters of Meadow Creek, and the trail will follow the creek through the canyon. It is approximately 11 miles to the point where Meadow Creek joins the Selway River. There are several good campgrounds at this juncture. Forest Road 443 dead-ends at Meadow Creek about 0.5 mile before it joins the Selway. Turn left along the Selway River and Selway Falls is approximately 1 mile ahead on your left.

Pioneer/White Knob Mountains   18

Location: North-central Idaho, 10 miles east of Ketchum.
Size: 120,000 acres.
Administration: USDAFS, Sawtooth and Challis National Forests.
Management status: Roadless, proposed wilderness.
Ecosystems: Middle Rocky Mountain steppe/coniferous forest/alpine meadow province characterized by complex and high, steep mountains; Precambrian granite, sedimentary, and volcanic rocks; Douglas fir forest type, with sagebrush steppe and smaller areas of alpine vegetation.
Elevation range: 7,169 feet at Lehman Butte to 12,009 feet at Hyndman Peak.
System trails: 79 miles.
Maximum core to perimeter distance: 25 miles.
Activities: Hiking, camping, fishing, and rock climbing.
Best months: July, August, and September.
Maps: Prophyry Peak-ID; Lehman Butte-ID; Mackay Reservoir-ID; Big Black Dome-ID; Copper Basin Knob-ID; Shelly Mtn.-ID; Big Blind Canyon-ID; Sun Valley-ID; Hyndman Peak-ID; Grays Peak-ID; Star Hope Mine-ID; Smiley Mtn.-ID; Miller Peak-ID; Grouse-ID; Appendicitis Hill-ID; Baugh Creek SW-ID; Baugh Creek-ID; Muldoon-ID; Trail Creek-ID; Blizzard Mountain North-ID; Champagne Creek-ID; Seaman's Creek-ID; Wood River Reservoir-ID; Lake Hills-ID; Fish Creek Reservoirs-ID (USGS 1:1,000,000).

OVERVIEW The Pioneer Mountain range is high and rugged and provides the eastern backdrop to the famous Sun Valley/Ketchum area. The Pioneers originate from rolling foothills at the valley's border and quickly rise to peaks with elevations around 10,000 feet. The White Knob Mountains lie to the northeast of the Pioneers and extend into the Lost River Valley. These mountains make a much more abrupt elevation gain than the Pioneers as they forgo the transition from foothills to peaks. However, with a maximum elevation of 11,278 feet at Shelly Mountain, they do not reach the elevations of the Pioneer Mountains.

Three distinct ranges and combination of ranges form what appear to be fingers stretching north to south over the east-central landscape of Idaho. The Pioneer Mountains lie at the extreme southern portion of the westernmost finger. The Lost River Valley lies to the east of the Pioneers, with the Lost River Mountains forming the second finger, followed by the Pahsimeroi Valley, the Lemhi Mountains, and the easternmost Lemhi Valley.

18 PIONEER/WHITE KNOB MOUNTAINS

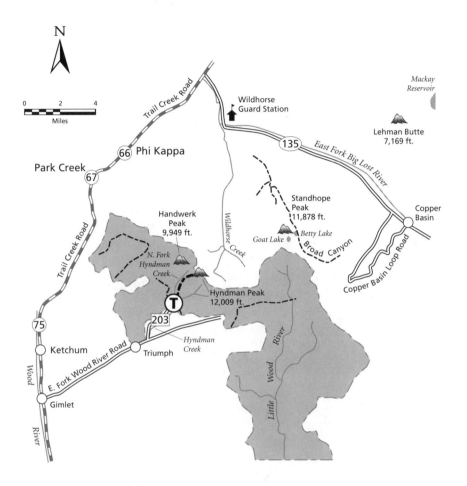

The Pioneer Mountains are largely arid but do offer varied terrain with interesting canyons among the peaks. Hyndman Creek and Little Wood River are among the streams that originate here and make their way to the Wood River to the south. The White Knobs are even drier and most of the streams and creeks in this vicinity are intermittent.

Like all of the mountains in this portion of the state, the Pioneers and White Knobs are high desert and the vegetation consists primarily of sagebrush and short native grasses. Underbrush is virtually nonexistent, and the peaks are bare granite. Pockets of forests lie mainly in protected canyons and mountain valleys. Summers are hot and dry, and winters are distinguished by a lot of wind, cold temperatures, and very little snowfall.

The lack of vegetation does not deter many species of large mammals from making their homes here, including pronghorn antelope, mule deer, cougar, mountain goat, and bighorn sheep.

RECREATIONAL USES Being close to the outdoor-conscious Sun Valley area to the west has its blessings and curses. The blessings are that the residents value their wild areas and are active in pushing for protection. They also take pride in helping to preserve the integrity of this roadless area and keep up maintenance on these trails. The curses are that they love them and tend to use them a lot. Therefore, some of the trails in the Pioneers and to a much lesser extent, the White Knobs, are apt to be quite busy at times, and mountain bikes are allowed throughout the system. The area is not designated as roadless, so motorized vehicles are allowed; and these users tend to utilize the trails closest to town. Therefore, it doesn't take long to leave these intrusions behind.

Mountain biking and hiking are the main pursuits, but fishing is also a very popular pastime as the small lakes in the Pioneer and White Knob Mountains contain a thriving native trout population.

Due to the largely bare landscape, excellent cross-country opportunities exist within these ranges. Many of the trails are accessible all winter, but care should be taken due to the extreme cold temperatures possible here. Several companies maintain yurts in the Pioneer Mountains for overnight camping. Contact the Sun Valley Chamber of Commerce for further information.

HOW TO GET THERE *Hyndman Peak:* From Ketchum drive 5 miles south to Gimlet on Idaho Highway 75. Turn left on East Fork Wood River Road and proceed 5 miles to Triumph. Just outside of Triumph turn left on Forest Road 203 and drive another 5 miles to the Hyndman Peak trailhead.

Day Hike

Hyndman Peak
Distance: 12 miles round-trip.
Difficulty: Strenuous.
Topo map: Hyndman Peak-ID.

This trail is very poor after the first few miles and very steep, with an elevation gain of 5,000 feet. That said, it is also a rewarding hike to the top of a peak that just exceeds 12,000 feet. There are awesome views of the surrounding country.

The Devil's Bedstead area can be accessed from the Hyndman Peak trail.

The trail heads east along the North Fork of Hyndman Creek for about 2 miles before starting to gain some serious elevation. You will be climbing to a ridgeline to the north and following the trail past a small pond and into a broad meadow. The trail becomes faint here, but the saddle of Hyndman Peak is now visible. Heading toward that saddle you will come across a small lake and the trail will cross at its outlet and then continue on past and above it. The last section to the summit involves climbing over and around a steep talus slope. There is a benchmark at the top.

Secesh/Payette Crest   19

Location: Western Idaho, 25 miles northeast of McCall.
Size: 227,678 acres.
Administration: USDAFS, Payette National Forest.
Management status: Wilderness.
Ecosystems: Middle Rocky Mountain coniferous forest/alpine meadow province, Idaho Batholith section, characterized by strongly glaciated mountains with cirques and U-shaped valleys; Douglas fir, western spruce-fir, and western ponderosa forest types with many perennial streams and high-elevation lakes.
Elevation range: 7,456 feet at Box Creek to 9,322 feet at North Loon Mountain.
System trails: 85 miles.
Maximum core to perimeter distance: 7 miles.
Activities: Hiking, fishing, and hunting.
Best months: July, August, and September.
Maps: Victor Peak-ID; Loon Lake-ID; Pony Meadows-ID; Pilot Peak-ID; Box Lake-ID; Enos Lake-ID; Fitsum Summit-ID; Fitsum Peak-ID; Paddy Flat-ID; Blackmare-ID (USGS 1:1,000,000).

OVERVIEW The Secesh/Payette Crest area is an expanse of land that is linked to the Gospel Hump Wilderness and the Frank Church–River of No Return Wilderness on their west sides. This area is part of the Salmon River Mountains and is essentially roadless, with Forest Service roads grouped mainly around the lower-elevation mountains on the west, from Rapid Creek to Warm Lake Road. The land is heavily forested, with deep canyons that have been carved by creeks coursing toward the Secesh River and the South Fork of the Salmon River. These creeks originate in numerous high-country lakes. These lakes and their resulting creeks provide spawning grounds for Idaho's endangered salmon and steelhead.

Abundant rainfall and the resulting lakes and streams provide lush vegetation in the form of dense forests and thick underbrush. These conditions provide prime habitat for wild game populations. Elk, white-tailed and mule deer, bear, and moose thrive in this climate and terrain. Numerous smaller species also enjoy the thick cover, including mountain lion, fox, marten, and several species of grouse.

RECREATIONAL USES Due to the impenetrability of its high ridges and dense forests, the Secesh/Payette Crest area has retained its wilderness characteristic. Except along the western edge overlooking McCall and the Cascade

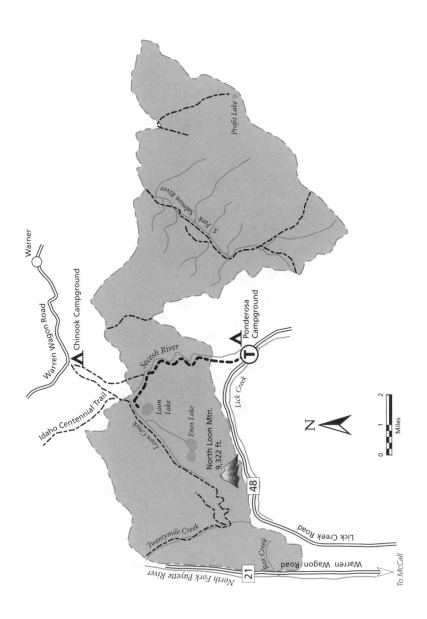

19B SECESH/PAYETTE CREST (FOOLHEN WAY TRAIL)

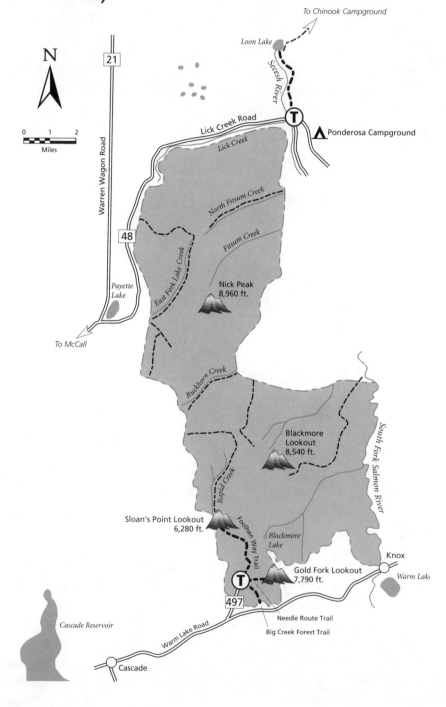

N

To Chinook Campground

Loon Lake

Secesh River

21

Warren Wagon Road

0 1 2
Miles

Lick Creek Road

Lick Creek

Ponderosa Campground

North Fitsum Creek

48

Fitsum Creek

East Fork Lake Creek

Payette Lake

Nick Peak
8,960 ft.

To McCall

Buckhorn Creek

Blackmore Lookout
8,540 ft.

South Fork Salmon River

Rapid Creek

Sloan's Point Lookout
6,280 ft.

Foolhen Way Trail

Blackmore Lake

Knox

Warm Lake

Gold Fork Lookout
7,790 ft.

497

Cascade Reservoir

Warm Lake Road

Needle Route Trail

Big Creek Forest Trail

Cascade

Reservoir, few roads intrude into this rugged landscape. These qualities make the area fantastic for solitary backcountry camping and hiking. Part of the attraction here is the opportunity to fish for wild, native trout species. Brook, bull, cutthroat, and rainbow trout are especially plentiful in the many small lakes and creeks feeding into the larger rivers. Hikes into these tiny lakes make for great fishing and destination trips.

The heavy underbrush confines hikers to the established trails, and plentiful winter precipitation may damage spring trails with downed timber and washouts. Many old Forest Service lookout towers are still in good condition, and easy-access hikes will provide great views.

The white water of the Secesh River and South Fork of the Salmon makes these rivers a popular destination for kayakers and rafters. The Secesh provides the truer wilderness experience, as there is a road that accompanies the South Fork of the Salmon alongside most of its length; the Secesh is escorted solely by a trail. That means a portage is necessary to access the Secesh River, but the lack of traffic makes it worth the haul. Several campsites are located alongside both rivers.

The lush vegetation that supports the larger animal species also draws numerous hunters into the backcountry each fall. Again, due to the lack of established roads, most traffic will be confined to areas with easier access, such as the Rapid Creek area. Traveling farther into the heart of the Secesh/Payette Crest will insure a purer wilderness experience.

HOW TO GET THERE *Secesh to Loon Lake:* From McCall take Lick Creek Road north 25 miles to the Ponderosa Campground and the trailhead.

Foolhen Way Trail: From Cascade take Warm Lake Road east for 10.5 miles. There will be a turnoff for Forest Road 497 and the Needles Route Trail. Follow this road 6 miles to the Gold Fork Lookout at an elevation of 7,790 feet.

Day Hike

Secesh to Loon Lake

Distance: 15 miles.
Difficulty: Easy.
Topo map: Loon Lake-ID.

This is a fairly easy hike through a canyon to beautiful Loon Lake and great camping and fishing.

The trail is part of the Idaho State Centennial Trail and crosses several small streams as it travels upstream along the Secesh River. The first few miles of the river can be kayaked down to Lick Creek, if you are willing to make the portage upstream. The river and trail lie within a somewhat narrow canyon for the first half of the hike before widening out into meadows as you gain elevation.

Loon Lake appears to the west and is a large lake in an open meadow encircled by forested mountains. It supports a good population of native trout and campsites can be made along the lake margins.

The trail continues north from here as it follows the Secesh River. It ends at the Chinook Campground off Warren Wagon Road.

Day Hike

Foolhen Way Trail

Distance: 15 miles round-trip.
Difficulty: Moderate.
Topo map: Sloans Point-ID; Gold Fork Rock-ID.

This trail provides excellent vantage points for viewing the Payette Crest area.

The Foolhen Way Trail starts from the Gold Fork lookout (before starting the hike, check out the views) and will travel roughly north for 12 miles to Sloan's Point Lookout at an elevation of 6,280 feet. This lookout provides an excellent view of the Payette Crest area to the northeast and of the Cascade Reservoir to the southwest. From the Sloan's Point Lookout backtrack to the point where Forest Road 401 crossed it. This road intersects with numerous other Forest Service roads that will exit the mountains.

Smoky Mountains

20

Location: Central Idaho, 10 miles west of Ketchum.
Size: 336,627 acres.
Administration: USDAFS, Sawtooth and Boise National Forests.
Management status: Roadless, nonwilderness.
Ecosystems: Middle Rocky Mountain steppe/coniferous forest/alpine meadow province, characterized by complex and high, steep mountains with sharp ridges and cirques; Precambrian granite and sedimentary and volcanic rock; Douglas fir forest type with sagebrush steppe and smaller areas of alpine vegetation.
Elevation range: 7,015 feet at Indian Head Rock to 10,285 feet at Norton Peak.
System trails: 168 miles.
Maximum core to perimeter distance: 12 miles.
Activities: Hiking, biking, fishing, hunting, and climbing.
Best months: July, August, and September.
Maps: Marshall Peak-ID; Frenchman Peak-ID; Galena-ID; Cayuse Point-ID; Ross Peak-ID; Newman Peak-ID; Paradise Peak-ID; Baker Peak-ID; Boardman Peak-ID; Sydney Butte-ID; Dollarhide Mtn.-ID; Buttercup Mtn.-ID (USGS 1:1,000,000).

OVERVIEW The Smoky Mountains have not yet been designated as wilderness; but they are a natural extension of the Sawtooth Wilderness to the north. These mountains are not as dramatic visually as the Sawtooths, and therefore they do not attract the same amount of backcountry use. And that is a large part of their appeal. While not as steep as the Sawtooth Mountains, the Smoky Mountains do contain many high, rugged peaks and rolling foothills sparsely covered with evergreens and sagebrush.

In the mid-1800s an ambitious mining district developed around the town of Atlanta, lying to the extreme northwest of the Smoky Mountains. Millions of dollars worth of gold and silver were mined and extracted, and evidence of some of this activity, including numerous one-lane roads, can be found on the west side of the Smoky Mountains.

The east side of the complex gets the most visitor use, as the resort towns of Sun Valley and Ketchum lie in that direction. The residents of these towns are avid recreationists, and the appeal of the Smokys are too good to resist. Many well-maintained trails originate near these towns and lead into the heart of the mountains. Though there is still evidence of old mining activity on the west side, few visitors travel here and it is well suited to solitary hiking.

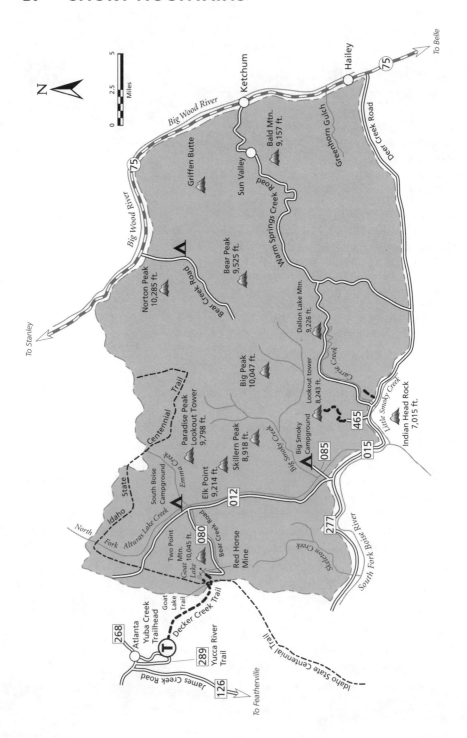

To Belle

Hailey

75

To Stanley

Ketchum

Big Wood River

Big Wood River

75

75

Griffen Butte

Sun Valley

Bald Mtn.
9,157 ft.

Greenhorn Gulch

Deer Creek Road

Warm Springs Creek Road

Bear Peak
9,525 ft.

Norton Peak
10,285 ft.

Bear Creek Road

Dallon Lake Mtn.
9,226 ft.

Carrie Creek

Big Peak
10,047 ft.

Lookout tower
8,243 ft.

Little Smoky Creek

Indian Head Rock
7,015 ft.

Paradise Peak
Lookout Tower
9,798 ft.

Centennial   Trail

Skillern Peak
8,918 ft.

465

Big Smoky Creek

Big Smoky
Campground

085

015

Idaho   State

South Boise
Campground

Emma   Creek

Elk Point
9,214 ft.

012

277

South Fork Boise River

North   Fork   Alturas Lake Creek

Two Point
Mtn.
10,045 ft.

Goat
Lake

Bear Creek Road

080

Red Horse
Mine

Skeleton Creek

Goat
Lake
Trail

Atlanta

268

Yuba Creek
Trailhead

T

Decker Creek Trail

289

Yucca River
Trail

James Creek Road

126

To Featherville

Idaho State Centennial Trail

N

5

2.5

0

Miles

The headwaters of the South Fork of the Boise River and the Big Wood River lie within the Smoky Mountains. These waters are fed by numerous springs, which insure that the area is fairly heavily vegetated, unlike the bare Sawtooths to the north.

The Smoky Mountains support a large variety of wildlife, including deer, elk, and black bear. The many creeks and streams provide excellent fishing with thriving populations of bull, brown, and rainbow trout as well as koka-nee salmon.

RECREATIONAL USES The Smoky Mountains are essentially roadless, but there are still a good number of old mining roads that access the interior. At-tempts have been made to include the Smoky Mountains under wilderness designation along with the Sawtooths, but so far that legislation has not come to pass. The area rises alongside Idaho Highway 75 on the east, but the ma-jority of backcountry traffic bypasses the Smokys for the Sawtooths.

The peaks are rugged, but the approaches to them lend themselves to hik-ing and horseback riding. Day hiking is common, and there are several good campgrounds located on forest routes. These campgrounds are close to excel-lent fishing on the main rivers in the system, particularly the South Fork of the Boise River, Big Smoky Creek, and Little Smoky Creek. The waterways in this system also support several good hot springs, which are a popular draw for local hikers.

The east side of the Smoky Mountains receive the most day use due to its proximity to the main road and the major towns of Sun Valley and Ketchum. To experience real solitude we recommend that hikers travel to the west side and the town of Atlanta.

HOW TO GET THERE *Decker Creek Trail:* From Atlanta take Forest Road 268 west 2 miles to Forest Road 289 (Yuba River) south. Travel 3.5 miles to the Yuba Creek trailhead.

Big Smoky Creek: From Featherville, south of Atlanta on the west side of the Smokys, take Forest Road 227 east for approximately 23 miles. This route fol-lows the South Fork of the Boise River, and there are many developed camp-grounds available along the road. At this point there is a junction, and you take Forest Road 085 north for 0.5 mile to the Big Smoky Campground.

Day Hike or Overnighter

Decker Creek Trail to Goat Lake

Distance: 11 miles round-trip.
Difficulty: Moderately strenuous.
Topo maps: Cayuse Point-ID; Ross Peak-ID.

Evidence of old mining history and a great campsite near excellent fishing make this a good hike.

From the Yuba Creek trailhead, take the Decker Creek Trail 6 miles south into Decker Canyon. The canyon starts off as a wide, open meadow and gradually narrows as the trail progresses. Here the trail will gain elevation as it crosses another broad meadow for about 1 mile. The trail will then drop down to the old Red Horse Mine, where it joins Bear Creek Road. Proceed on Bear Creek Road for 2.5 miles and turn off at the Goat Lake Trail. Hiking uphill another 2 miles will bring you to Goat Lake. Caution should be used around old mine sites as they are not maintained.

Day Hike or Overnighter

Big Smoky Creek

Distance: 3 miles round-trip.
Difficulty: Moderate.
Topo map: Sydney Butte-ID.

This hike involves driving between locations, but it's like a smorgasbord: You get a taste for the area's excellent fishing, a hot-springs soak, and a hike to a great vantage point that makes it well worth the effort.

From Big Smoky Campground there is a trail that follows Big Smoky Creek upstream for 1 mile to a campsite and the opportunity for fishing wild bull and rainbow trout and kokanee salmon.

Backtrack the trail and get on Forest Road 227 once again (see previous directions in "How to Get There"). Turn left and continue for 5 miles, making a left on Forest Road 015. Follow this road for 1 mile to the Smoky Hot Springs. These warm waters are worth a good, long visit.

From the Hot Springs turn right on Forest Road 465 and follow it to the end. From here a 0.5-mile trail leads north to a good Forest Service lookout tower. At 8,243 feet this is a great vantage point for viewing the Big Smoky Creek drainage and the surrounding Smoky Mountains.

South-Central: Desert Highlands

Great Rift Backcountry Area

21

Location: Southeast Idaho, 45 miles east of Idaho Falls.
Size: 180 square miles (excluding Craters of the Moon National Monument).
Administration: BLM.
Management status: Proposed wilderness, National Natural Landmark at Hell's Half Acre.
Ecosystems: Intermountain semidesert province; semi-arid and cool, characterized by sagebrush steppes and extensive lava flows; sagebrush and shad scale supported, along with short grasses.
Elevation range: 4,590 feet at Shale Butte to 5,261 feet at Pillar Butte.
System trails: 1 mile of designated trail at Hell's Half Acre.
Maximum core to perimeter distance: 18 miles.
Activities: Hiking and exploring.
Best months: March and April.
Maps: Woodville-ID; Morgans Pasture NE-ID; Nichols Reservoir-ID; Arco South-ID; Inferno Cone-ID; The Watchman-ID; Fingers Butte-ID; Paddleford Flat-ID; Little Park-ID; North Laidlaw Butte-ID; Fissure Butte-ID; Pratt Butte-ID; Pagari Well-ID; Wagon Butte-ID; Laidlaw Butte-ID; Bear Park West-ID; Bear Park East-ID; Black Ridge Crater-ID; Halfway Lake-ID; Laidlaw Lake-ID; Bear Park SW-ID; Mule Butte-ID; Owinza-ID; Senter-ID; Shale Butte-ID; Pillar Butte-ID; Pillar Butte NE-ID; Schoodle Well-ID; Rattlesnake Butte-ID; Pillar Butte SE-ID; Gifford Spring-ID; Register Rock-ID (USGS 1:1,000,000).

OVERVIEW On November 8, 2000, the Craters of the Moon National Monument boundary was greatly expanded. This chapter focuses on the Great Rift backcountry area. Chapter 22, "Craters of the Moon National Monument," focuses on the original boundary. Though the backcountry's flow is now within the main monument, it is south of and somewhat divorced from the main lava flow. The expansion of the boundary now encompasses all of the huge lava flow that extends over much of south-central Idaho. The flow is the result of volcanic activity that ended approximately 2,000 to 5,200 years ago. This makes the flow truly unique, as it is a relatively "fresh" flow, and much of its original characteristics have been preserved. The flow stretches over 65 miles north to south from the town of Arco to American Falls. Volcanic eruptions originated in the area of what is now known as the Craters of the Moon National Monument near Arco, and the lava subsequently spread south and east. This huge expanse of lava is largely untracked and can reach depths of 800 feet. The area displays fascinating terrain consisting of buttes, craters, cinder and spatter

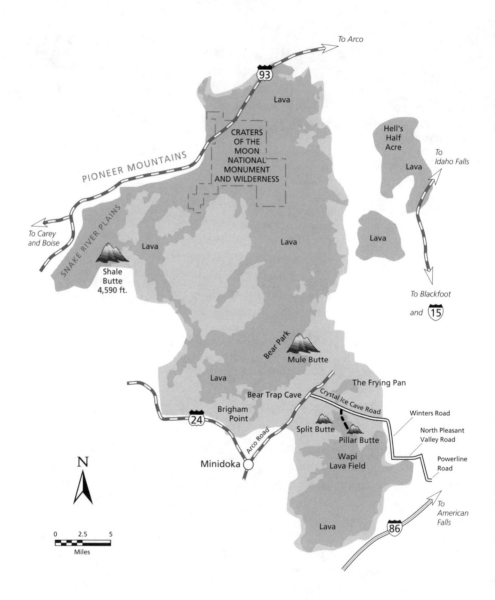

cones, calderas, spires, and lava tubes. Some of the caves in this area are known to have been inhabited by primitive peoples as early as A.D. 1200.

According to one theory, the explanation for this distinctive geological feature is that the Yellowstone Plateau, where the cluster of geysers and hotpots are located in Yellowstone National Park, marks the current location of a "hotspot" in the earth's upper mantle. The buttes and lava fields of Idaho's Snake River Plain are the remnants and traces of the hotspot's northeastward track across the North American Plate. According to this theory then, the hotspot is still migrating northeast and the unique features of Yellowstone will eventually cease.

Though conditions appear to be harsh and forbidding, wildlife find the area a good refuge; sage grouse, mourning doves, mule deer, and pronghorn antelope call this place home.

Vegetation does not flourish in the lava fields, but sagebrush, antelope bitterbush, cedar, mockorange, and tansybush grow sparsely in the pockets of soil that have been blown into crevasses of the lava.

RECREATIONAL USES The lava flows of Idaho provide a truly unique experience for hikers. The sharp volcanic rock and deep crevasses keep all other outdoor users out of this forbidding country, allowing hikers complete solitude.

Caves, tunnels, and crevasses provide challenging exploration in this trailless landscape. New features are still being discovered, since most people have not made the effort to venture past the few established trails. Due to its relatively small size and easy access from nearby roads, the Hell's Half Acre lava flow is a good introduction to exploring this type of country. The flow actually sits like an island in a sea of farm ground, making orientation easier for hikers.

From the Craters of the Moon National Monument, the origination point of this volcanic activity, two fingerlike lava fields flow southward. The western field extends from the town of Carey south to I–24. This section has several roads transecting in the southern half, but the northern section is completely "wild." From the southeastern tip of Craters of the Moon National Monument, the other field flows south for 18 miles. This area contains absolutely no roads. The Wapi Lava Field lies across a narrow plain and to the southeast. The Hell's Half Acre flow, one of the smaller flows, is isolated and unconnected to the bigger sections.

Hiking is the only recreational activity in the flows due to the extremely rough terrain and the lack of designated trails. The opportunity to experience these unique geological formations and enjoy true solitude is unsurpassed here but should be explored with adequate maps, compass, water supply, and a healthy dose of respect. This place has gone largely unexplored, and due to its inherent inaccessibility, new features will continue to be discovered here for years to come.

HOW TO GET THERE *Hell's Half Acre:* 16 miles southwest of Idaho Falls on I–15, going south toward Blackfoot. Access is right off the highway at an Idaho Transportation Department rest stop.

Pillar Butte: From American Falls take Powerline Road north for 5 miles to North Pleasant Valley Road and turn left. This road ends after 11 miles, and you continue north on Winters Road for 3.5 miles. Turn left on Crystal Ice Cave Road and travel 2 miles to parking and the edge of the lava flow.

Day Hike

Hell's Half Acre

Distance: I mile round-trip.
Difficulty: Easy.
Topo Maps: Woodville-ID.

This hike is an easy way to experience the drama of this stark landscape. The trail features paved walkways originating at the Idaho Transportation Department rest stop and leads through the lava flow with only gentle inclines. There are numerous interpretive signs along the trail that highlight the unusual aspects of this terrain and also describe the wildlife and vegetation that the area supports.

There is another very good interpretive trail located behind the northbound I–15 Blackfoot rest area.

Day Hike

Pillar Butte

Distance: 8 miles round-trip.
Difficulty: Moderate.
Topo maps: Pillar Butte SE.

This hike to the summit of Pillar Butte is not on an established trail but offers solitude and a great view of the south lying Wapi Lava Field. Early travelers on the Oregon Trail valued this butte as a landmark, and it remains a distinctive feature in the vast and primarily flat landscape of the Snake River Plain.

Pillar Butte lies at the northernmost portion of the main Wapi Lava Field; access is reached by parking at the end of Crystal Ice Cave Road and walking in. As mentioned earlier there is no established trail, but walking is fairly easy due to the smooth *pahoehoe* (smooth lava) found here. The climb to the summit, at 5,261 feet, is gradual.

Craters of the Moon
National Monument

22

Location: Southeast Idaho, 18 miles west of Arco.
Size: 700,000 acres.
Administration: NPS, BLM, National Monument.
Management status: Wilderness, roadless.
Ecosystems: Intermountain semidesert province; semi-arid and cool, characterized by sagebrush steppes and extensive lava flows; sagebrush and shad scale supported, along with short grasses.
Elevation range: 5,989 feet at Crescent Butte to 6,516 feet at Big Cinder Butte.
System trails: 7 miles.
Maximum core to perimeter distance: 12 miles.
Activities: Hiking, backpacking, cross-country skiing (on Scenic Loop Drive), and caving.
Best months: March and April; January for cross-country skiing.
Maps: Inferno Cone-ID; The Watchman-ID (USGS 1:1,000,000); Craters of the Moon Visitor's Map.

OVERVIEW Craters of the Moon National Monument lies at the center of the Great Rift Zone of volcanic activity that extends more than 65 miles, from the town of Arco in the north to American Falls in the south. On November 8, 2000, the Craters of the Moon National Monument was expanded to include all of this unique area. (See chapter 21, "Great Rift Backcountry Area," for more information.) Lava began erupting here roughly 15,000 years ago and ceased about 2,500 years ago. That makes this flow quite young in geological time. Spatter cones, tube caves, and cinder cones dot a landscape so harsh that much of the area still remains unexplored. Two distinct types of lava, 'a'a and pahoehoe, are distributed throughout the park. 'a'a, the Hawaiian generic term for lava, is described as very rough and sharp. 'a'a lava forms as a result of fast lava flows usually over steep slopes. The fast moving fluid causes variable cooling rates, which causes the lava to crack and fold up over itself leaving behind a jagged landscape. Pahoehoe means "smooth lava" in Hawaiian and is a result of a much slower flow rate, generally over a flatter terrain. This flow leaves behind smooth lava with ropy formations.

The Shoshone avoided it, covered wagons detoured around it, and miners steered clear of this land that had been called "a desolate and awful waste." The area was finally explored in 1920 when two men, Robert Limbert and W. L. Cole, and their dog traveled 28 miles on foot through what is now the entire

22   CRATERS OF THE MOON
NATIONAL MONUMENT

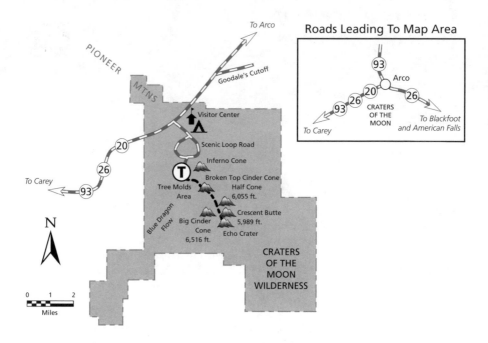

monument and wilderness. The pair suffered through sleeplessness, lack of water, and blisters but were still so awed by this landscape that their support of it, in the forms of notes and photographs, was instrumental in securing National Monument status in 1924. Mr. Limbert wrote: "The 'Valley of the Moon' lies in a region literally combed with underground caves and passages, bewildering in their immensity, mystifying in their variety of strange formations, where there are natural bridges as yet unknown to geographers, where bear tracks hundreds of years old may be traced for miles across cinder flats. Here are craters of dormant volcanoes half a mile wide and seemingly bottomless, huge cups in which the five-story Owyhee hotel might be placed to resemble a lone sugar loaf in a huge bowl. Here are strange ice caves with stalactites and ice-encrusted walls, caves that contain as much ice in the middle of August as they do in the winter." (Robert Limbert Collection, Boise State University). Wilderness does not get any 'wilder' than that.

The northern section of the monument played a part in the greatest migration in U.S. history: Migrants followed the Oregon Trail through Idaho to the verdant lands that awaited them in Oregon and California. This route followed the course of the Snake River about 100 miles south of the current monument.

In 1862 a wagon train guide named Tim Goodale led a train northwest from Fort Hall, Idaho, on a little-used cutoff. Goodale's entourage made it safely into the Oregon Territory and his route—known as Goodale's Cutoff—became the dominant one as hostilities between travelers and Native Americans heated up on the more southerly Oregon Trail. Goodale's Cutoff lies approximately 6 miles northwest of the Craters of the Moon visitor center; more information is available there on how to trace this route.

The monument maintains only 7 miles of trail, but the Craters of the Moon can be explored much farther into the wilderness area. A free permit is issued to backcountry travelers. Park officials warn that the 'a'a lava that extends to the south becomes so abrasive and cutting that travel becomes extremely difficult. Water is scarce and undependable, and although some of the deep fissure vents contain snowmelt and ice year-round they are quite difficult to locate. Artifacts of the Northern Shoshoni have been found in the wilderness and include temporary shelters and hunting blinds. These items are protected and should be admired and then left in their natural state.

Though the landscape is harsh and seemingly untenable, it supports more than 2,000 insect species, 148 birds, 47 mammals, 8 reptiles, and a lone amphibian, the western toad. Mule deer, bobcat, and great horned owl also make a home here.

The predominant vegetation is sagebrush and short grasses, although a total of more than 300 plant species can be found clinging to the scant soil pockets deposited in lava fissures.

RECREATIONAL USES Hiking and exploring are the main activities throughout the Craters system. Scenic Loop Road is closed in winter but opened to and groomed for cross-country skiers.

Caving is the great attraction, with new and undiscovered systems being found in the backcountry on a regular basis. Strong flashlights, sturdy boots, a compass, and extra fluids are recommended when exploring this mostly arid country.

Hikers venturing into the Craters of the Moon Wilderness in the southeastern section of the monument are advised to notify the ranger of their travel plans. The lava is extremely abrasive and treacherous, the water virtually nonexistent, and the caves very dark. The temptation is great, but collecting rocks and other artifacts is strictly prohibited.

The visitors center lies at the entrance to the monument and is open daily. It contains displays on the natural and human history of the area, as well as a short video that describes the volcanic geology of the monument. Adjacent to the visitors center is a well-maintained campground with full facilities.

The shorter designated trails in the monument are paved and offer excellent handicapped access. These trails explore the cinder cones and lava tube caves and range from 0.5 mile to 7 miles in length.

Bicycling is allowed, and only possible, on Scenic Loop Road and on Goodale's Cutoff. Goodale's Cutoff lies at the northern region of the park.

HOW TO GET THERE *Tree Molds Area:* From Arco follow Idaho Highway 20, 26, and 93 west 18 miles to the Craters of the Moon visitor center. From the visitors center follow the Craters of the Moon Loop Road to the right to a spur road just beyond Inferno Cone, and follow that for 2 miles to access the trailhead at the Tree Molds area parking lot.

Echo Crater: The trailhead is 75 yards southeast of the Tree Molds area parking lot on Craters of the Moon Loop Road.

Day Hike

Tree Molds Area

Distance: 3 miles round-trip.
Difficulty: Easy.
Topo map: Inferno Cone.

This is a really easy hike that highlights some of the unique features in this area. The trail winds through shrubs and stands of pine before reaching the edge of the Blue Dragon Flow. The area is noted for the tree molds that formed when liquid lava surrounded and encased standing trees. The lava eventually hardened and the tree inside rotted, leaving these fascinating molds. The molds, which range in size from a few inches to 3 feet in diameter, are found at the end of this hike.

Day Hike

Echo Crater

Distance: 6 miles round-trip.
Difficulty: Moderate.
Topo map: Inferno Cone-ID.

This is another fairly easy trail, one which features some of the caves and buttes that characterize the area. It travels up and over the Broken Top cinder cone before descending onto the most recent lava flow in the monument. The trail continues past Big Cinder Butte to a grove of lava trees and fissures that lies to the west of the trail. It continues between Coyote and Crescent Buttes and then leads to Echo Crater. Numerous caves are accessible and explorable from the trail.

Mount Borah
23

Location: Central Idaho, 21 miles north of Mackay.
Size: 116,500 acres.
Administration: USDAFS, Challis National Forest.
Management status: Proposed roadless.
Ecosystems: Middle Rocky Mountain steppe/coniferous forest/alpine meadow province characterized by complex and high, steep mountains; Precambrian granite and sedimentary and volcanic rock; Douglas fir forest type with sagebrush steppe and smaller areas of alpine vegetation.
Elevation range: 7,240 feet at the base to 12,662 feet at Borah Peak.
System trails: 35 miles.
Maximum core to perimeter distance: 15 miles.
Activities: Hiking, rock climbing, and picnicking.
Best months: July and August.
Maps: Grouse Creek Mtn.-ID; Doublespring-ID; Dickey Mtn.-ID; Borah Peak-ID; Burnt Creek-ID; Elkhorn Creek-ID; Leatherman Peak-ID; Massacre Mtn.-ID; Mackay-ID (USGS 1:1,000,000).

OVERVIEW Rising majestically from the floor of the Lost River Valley, Mount Borah commands attention as the centerpiece of the Lost River Mountain range. As Idaho's highest peak, it rises straight from the valley floor to its full 12,662 feet. Alongside it, eight other summits also surpass 12,000 feet in elevation. These mountains are sparsely forested and therefore provide ample opportunity to study the area's geology.

Mount Borah was named after Senator William Borah, a strong and early advocate for wilderness preservation in Idaho.

Mount Borah made a place for itself in Idaho history when a massive earthquake struck here on October 28, 1983. Early in the morning an earthquake that registered with a magnitude of 7.3 on the Richter scale ripped through the Lost River Valley. Homes and businesses in the nearby towns of Mackay and Challis were damaged and two lives were lost. The quake had originated at the base of Mount Borah, leaving a massive fault line 21 miles long and up to 14 feet deep that significantly lowered the valley floor and pushed the mountains to even higher elevations. An historical marker, located at the parking lot at the base of the mountain, describes the event and the geological features that resulted from it.

23 MOUNT BORAH

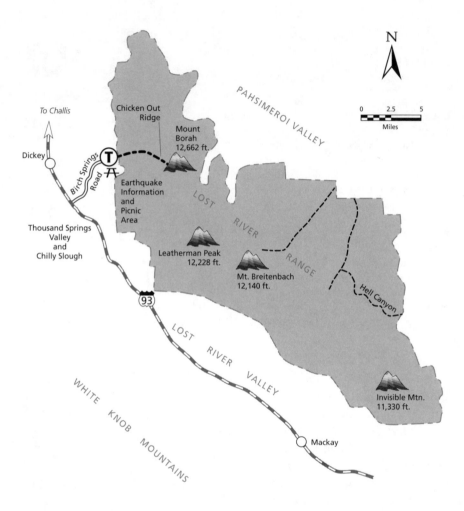

The mountain's other claim to fame is its glacier—the only one in Idaho. It is located on Mount Borah's north side.

As is common in this arid area of the state, the mountainside is largely bare, with sagebrush and short grasses predominating. Existing forests lie mostly in the protected canyons between peaks. Although dry, the area does support an impressive number of big game species including pronghorn antelope and moose at lower elevations and cougar, mountain goat, and bighorn sheep at the higher elevations.

RECREATIONAL USES Mount Borah and the mountains surrounding it do not currently have protected status. Due to the geology here, which includes huge expanses of bare ground, off-road use by dirt bikes, four-wheelers, and snowmachines is prevalent. In fact signs of this use are quite obvious, and trails can easily be seen from the road. The areas denied this use are those that are inherently too steep to make travel possible. Therefore even if at some point the area is granted protected status, it will take much monitoring to enforce the restrictions.

Due to the steepness of its slopes, Mount Borah is protected from lots of visitors. The mountain presents a good opportunity to view the surrounding area unbothered as well as to attain the highest summit in Idaho. It is also a great place to view recent geology as the fault line created in the 1983 earthquake is visible as a miles-long, deep scar running along the base of the mountain range. The area is still under study by the United States Geological Survey as earthquakes are still frequently recorded.

Mount Borah overlooks another unique geological feature in this otherwise parched landscape: Chilly Slough in the Thousand Springs Valley to the southwest. This area encompasses 5,000 acres of wetlands in the midst of the vast high-country desert. The Chilly Slough Wetland Conservation Project was put in place to protect 1,462 of those acres and to make the wetlands accessible for canoeing, wildlife viewing, and fishing. As an oasis in the desert, the wetlands provide habitat for 134 different type of birds, including sandhill crane, golden eagle, trumpeter swan, and peregrine falcon. Plant species particular to the Chilly Slough include cattail, manna-grass, watercress, and pondweed.

HOW TO GET THERE *Borah Peak*: From MacKay take U.S. Highway 93 north for 21 miles. Turn off on the road marked BIRCH SPRINGS ROAD—ACCESS TO MT. BORAH, heading east for about 2 miles until you reach the base of the mountain. There are primitive camping facilities here as well as an interpretive site.

To Chilly Slough: Follow the directions above, except at the turnoff for Birch Springs Road turn left (west) toward Chilly. Proceed 2 miles and there will be a sign directing you to a turnoff for wildlife viewing.

Day Hike

Borah Peak

Distance: 7 miles round-trip.
Difficulty: Strenuous and hazardous at summit.
Topo map: Borah Peak-ID.

The climb to the summit is very hard due to the quick elevation gain and tough scramble at Chicken Out Ridge. However, the hike is well worth the effort as it provides a spectacular view of the surrounding mountains and the Lost River Valley as well as the opportunity to bag a summit.

The trail begins at the end of Birch Springs Road and climbs gradually as it follows the canyon as it progresses along the south side of the mountain. Approximately 2 miles up the trail the hike becomes much harder as the trail quickly gains elevation on its ascent up a ridge on the west. The trail evens out as it follows the ridgeline just before Chicken Out Ridge. This ridge was so named because it is the point where some hikers decide to turn around and head back down the trail. This section is very steep and can be quite dangerous as it's an actual hand and foot scramble.

Once past Chicken Out Ridge the trail fades out, but it is now simple to follow the ridgeline to the visible summit.

Lemhi Mountains   24

Location: East-central Idaho, 20 miles south of Salmon.
Size: 408,000 acres.
Administration: USDAFS, Salmon and Targhee National Forests.
Management status: Roadless, proposed wilderness.
Ecosystems: Middle Rocky Mountain steppe/coniferous forest/alpine meadow province characterized by complex and high, steep mountains; Precambrian granite and sedimentary and volcanic rock; Douglas fir forest type with sagebrush steppe and smaller areas of alpine vegetation.
Elevation range: 8,470 feet at the base of Sheephorn Peak to 12,197 feet at Diamond Peak.
System trails: 109 miles.
Maximum core to perimeter distance: 7 miles.
Activities: Hiking, exploring, fishing, and hunting.
Best months: June and July.
Maps: Allison Peak-ID; Lem Peak-ID; May NW-ID; May NE-ID; Patterson NW-ID; Mat SE-ID; Patterson SW-ID; Patterson SE-ID; Donkey Hills NW-ID; Donkey Hills NE-ID; Gilmore NW-ID; Gilmore NE-ID; Donkey Hills SE-ID; Gilmore SW-ID; Gilmore SE-ID; Nicholia SW-ID; Hawley Mtn. SE-ID; Diamond Peak NW-ID; Diamond Peak NE-ID; Diamond Peak SW-ID; Diamond Peak SE-ID; Eightmile Canyon-ID; Howe NE-ID; Tyler Peak-ID (USGS 1:1,000,000).

OVERVIEW The Lemhi Mountains are a narrow, 100-mile-long range that divides the Lemhi and Pahsimeroi River Valleys. To the east lies the Great Divide and to the west lies the Lost River Range, which contains Mount Borah, Idaho's highest peak.

From May Mountain in the north to Tyler Peak in the south, these mountains are very steep and heavily forested on the peaks and in the canyon breaks. The peaks, especially to the south, rise dramatically from the high-desert valleys. The rough terrain has discouraged road-building beyond what is already in place from previous mining activity. Consequently, the areas that have roads in place are the ones that are used, and the rest of the range remains largely untraveled.

The Lemhi Mountains were named for the tribe of Native Americans who inhabited this area, the Lemhis. The name of the tribe, a branch of the Shoshone, came about when Mormon settlers entered the valley in 1855 and built Fort Limhi. The name stuck, but the settlers were driven from the area three years later by the Bannock tribe.

24   LEMHI MOUNTAINS

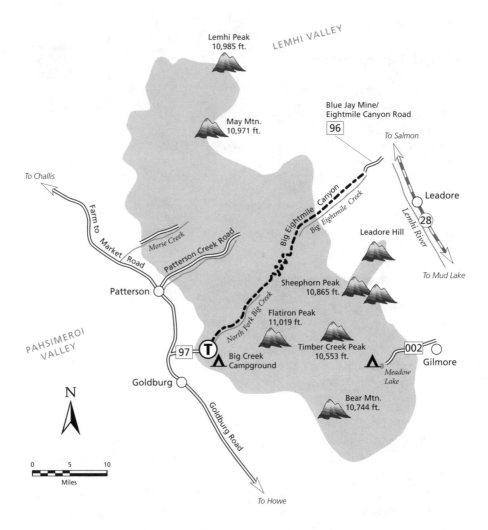

The Lemhis were the people of the guide Sacagawea, who led the Lewis and Clark expedition on their search for an alternate route to the Pacific Ocean. The expedition entered the valley from Lemhi Pass in the Beaverhead Mountains to the east and stayed with the tribe while investigating the trail to the north along the Salmon River. Many sites in the area show archaeological evidence of habitation by this tribe, and there is a monument to Sacagawea in the town of Tendoy. (More information on the Lewis and Clark expedition is in the Introduction.)

Mining activities in these mountains were extensive until approximately 1940 and are evidenced by numerous abandoned mines and miner's homesteads. The area was so productive at one point that mining towns sprang up throughout the surrounding mountains. The ghost town of Gilmore, south of the town of Leadore and in the foothills of the Lemhis, provides mute testimony to the mining heritage of the area. Following Forest Road 002, which angles south of Gilmore and heads farther west into the mountains, you will come upon the remains of a large mine that once provided employment for the residents of Gilmore. Other evidence of mining activity in the area includes brick charcoal kilns and visible reforestation of the strip logging that fed those kilns. Extracted ore was transported to the valley floor, where it was shipped by rail to outlying markets. Evidence of the abandoned railroad bed is still visible south of the town of Leadore. Few of these artifacts have maintained road access at this time; the notable exceptions being sites that are considered to have historic value, specifically the charcoal kilns off Idaho Highway 28. Therefore, hiking the old miners' trails in the Lemhis can provide fairly easy traveling as well as archaeological interest.

Wildlife, especially elk and black bear, is abundant in these mountains, and the ruggedness of the terrain provides adequate protection from seasonal hunters. Other species include Canada-transplanted endangered gray wolf, pronghorn antelope, deer, grouse, moose, cougar, mountain goat, and bighorn sheep. High-mountain lakes, rivers, and streams support native trout populations; many of these waters host hatchery transplants.

The Lemhi Valley is arid and primarily supports sagebrush and native wild grasses. Farmland exists along the valley floor and extends upward until the mountains take over. At this point the vegetation becomes heavily forested with very little underbrush.

The Lemhi Mountains trap most of the precipitation that enters the area, so the intervening valleys remain extremely arid, with wind being the predominant weather feature.

RECREATIONAL USES The Lemhi Mountains and Lemhi Valley have a long human history. The combination of plentiful game in the mountains and mild summer temperatures made this a popular camp for the Lemhi Indians. Sacagawea, the guide for the Lewis and Clark expedition, was born into this tribe. When the expedition reached the valley, Sacagawea's people helped them travel north to find a passage west. Many historical sites and markers in the valley mark their passage.

The headwaters of the Lemhi River are especially important, as they serve as spawning grounds for salmon. These fish have traveled upriver from the Salmon River to these quiet backwaters to lay their eggs.

The mountains form startling images within the vast expanse of the Lemhi Valley.

In the 1800s, Idaho's central mountains were discovered to be rich in mineral resources. A fortune in nickel, silver, and lead was pulled from these mountains, and numerous towns and camps were built in the canyons to supply the miners' needs. Many of these towns and cabins are still standing and can be accessed by four-wheel-drive vehicles on precarious one-lane roads or by hiking on abandoned roads. Small mines and shafts dot the landscape; extreme care should be exercised when venturing near these sites. Several spots in the valley also have preserved beehive-type charcoal kilns and make for an interesting archaeological stop. Old clear-cut marks can be seen in some sections: the source for the charcoal at the kilns.

Today, these mountains see mostly day use by sightseers and picnickers. Several beautiful cirque lakes are easy to reach, such as Meadow Lake, via maintained access roads, and campgrounds have been established near them. Foot and four-wheel-drive traffic pick up during the hunting season as deer and elk populations are very numerous in this area. This traffic centers around the precarious mining roads; human incursion into the backcountry is limited as the terrain becomes harder to navigate the farther in you go. However, the farther back you go, the more you'll be rewarded. Steep and heavily forested peaks drop into deep valleys and numerous beautiful lakes dot the landscape.

HOW TO GET THERE *North Fork, Big Creek Trail:* The trail starts at the Big Creek Campground, which is reached by turning north from the town of Howe on Goldburg Road and driving 57 miles until you see the sign for Big Creek Trail. It is another 3.5 miles to the campground and trailhead.

Day Hike

North Fork, Big Creek Trail

Distance: 13 miles one way.
Difficulty: Easy to moderate.
Topo maps: Eightmile Canyon-ID; Patterson SE-ID; Donkey Hills NE-ID.

This trail provides an easy hike to scenic vistas and pretty waterfalls. The trail is little used, but be aware that some of that use is in the form of off-road vehicles toward the end of the hike in Eightmile Canyon.

From the trailhead you stay to the left as the trail follows the North Fork of Big Creek into a deep canyon. The trail follows the creek for 8 miles with minimal elevation gain. Along the way there are many small waterfalls that drop down from the canyon walls to spill into Big Creek.

At the end of the canyon the trail climbs slightly and then annexes the Big Eightmile Creek Trail. The combined trail then switchbacks as it climbs the mountains before dropping down into the Big Eightmile Creek drainage. Five miles after joining with the Big Eightmile Trail the trail ends at Forest Road 96 and the old Blue Jay Mine. Forest Road 96 leads to Idaho Highway 28 and Leadore.

Cache Crest/Mount Naomi

25

Location: Southeast Idaho, 10 miles west of Bloomington.
Size: 42,491 acres, Cache Crest; 28,077 acres, Mount Naomi (USDAFS).
Administration: USDAFS, Caribou National Forest.
Management status: Roadless, proposed wilderness (16,000 acres, Cache Crest; 14,600 acres, Mount Naomi).
Ecosystems: Intermountain semidesert province characterized by high, rolling plateaus and sagebrush steppe with smaller areas of alpine vegetation. Mountains are dominated by juniper woodlands, sagebrush, and grassland. In the alpine areas ponderosa pine generally occupies the lower and more exposed slopes and Douglas fir the higher and more sheltered ones.
Elevation range: 6,400 feet at Litz Basin to 9,575 feet at Paris Peak.
System trails: 82 miles.
Maximum core to perimeter distance: 5 miles.
Activities: Hiking, camping, fishing, and hunting.
Best months: April and May.
Maps: Mink Creek-ID; Paris Peak-ID; Paris-ID; Mapleton-ID; Egan Basin-ID; St. Charles-ID (USGS 1:1,000,000).

OVERVIEW The country due east of U.S. Highway 15 is a surprise to those who have taken the time to discover it. Viewed from the highway the landscape appears dry and barren—a flat and unappealing desert that seems to stretch forever. But venture farther east and you find an oasis of wooded mountains and buttes that rise off the desert floor, standing alone and unconnected to any others.

Cache Crest (known to the locals as Worm Creek) and Mount Naomi lie within the combined Wasatch and Bear River Mountain Ranges and are a continuation of the Wasatch–Cache National Forest in north-central Utah. These lands are also extensions of designated wilderness areas just over the border in Utah. The lands south of the Snake River are desert country and notably arid; the Wasatch/Bear River Ranges mark the end of that type of terrain. Here the mountains rise out of the sage flatlands and are soon carpeted with evergreens. On their eastern flanks the mountains drop off into a totally different landscape: The immense Bear Lake and its feeder streams as well as the Dingle Swamp lie within this great basin.

25 CACHE CREST/MOUNT NAOMI

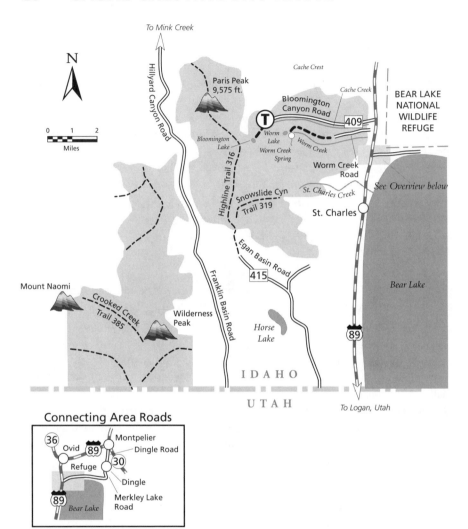

The Wasatch/Bear River Ranges, being the highest and lushest country for many miles, have attracted and supported large populations of animals more common to northern areas. Elk and moose, mountain lion, black bear, and beaver all reside within these ranges.

RECREATIONAL USES Its cousin to the south (in Utah) is protected by wilderness designation, but the Idaho side of Wasatch–Cache National Forest has not yet followed suit. Developers have little interest in Cache Crest/Mount

Naomi, but as an oasis in the generally parched southern plains it is very attractive to a wide variety of recreational users. Hunting is quite popular in the fall as the mountain lion population here is thriving, and so the area draws hunters into the region. Bear, elk, deer, and moose are also plentiful.

The great Bear Lake lies to the east of the range and is an impressive sight from many of the peaks in the area. Feeding into the lake from the north is an immense system of streams, creeks, and swamps. This area is protected as the Bear Lake National Wildlife Refuge and provides sanctuary for more than 161 species of birds, including the rare ibis, northern harrier, whooping crane, and peregrine falcon. The refuge is well worth a stop in early spring to view the migratory birds coming in. The refuge can be reached by taking Dingle Road south from the town of Dingle. Dingle Road turns into Merkley Lake Road after 2 miles, and you continue on this road for an additional 6 miles. Here the road will turn right and you follow it across the outlet; Bear Lake will be on your left and the refuge on your right. Just over 3 miles past the bridge a road heads to the right, due north, for a 4-mile drive through the refuge and into the back part of the town of Bloomington.

Because Bear Lake is such a popular destination in the summer months, the Cache Crest/Mount Naomi roadless area suffers some of the overflow of visitors. Though most people attempt to stay in close proximity of the lake, the St. Charles Creek drainage to the south of the Cache Crest area is a popular destination as it is an access point to the Minnetonka Cave. The Minnetonka Cave is a vast limestone cavern with many rooms, and tours are conducted daily.

Due to its location on the border of Utah, where it continues south and becomes wilderness, Mount Naomi is the more remote of the two areas. Few access roads lead into the area, and several trails head southward into Utah and thus farther into protected wilderness and solitude.

HOW TO GET THERE *Bloomington Lake:* From Bloomington take Bloomington Canyon Road west 10 miles to the Bloomington Canyon trailhead.

Worm Lake: Just over 1 mile south of Bloomington take the Worm Creek Road west for 3 miles to the trailhead.

Day Hike

Bloomington Lake

Distance: 0.5-mile round-trip.
Difficulty: Easy.
Topo maps: Paris Peak-ID.

The east side of Bear Lake.

Bloomington Lake lies at an elevation of 8,200 feet and is notable as a great fishing spot. The lake is easily accessible and therefore quite popular, but it is still worth a quick trip. Bloomington Lake encompasses ten acres and has a very healthy population of rainbow, brown, and cutthroat trout.

The lake is accessed by driving up Bloomington Canyon Road and parking at the trailhead parking lot. The access road and trailhead facilities are in the process of being improved, and the lake is still only accessible by foot.

Day Hike

Worm Lake

Distance: 10 miles round-trip.
Difficulty: Moderately strenuous.
Topo map: Paris Peak-ID.

This is another opportunity for great fishing but on a trail and at a location that offers much more solitude. The hike starts at an old mine site and follows the Worm Creek drainage up into the mountains. The trail connects with several others, but Worm Creek Trail travels almost exclusively west. Approximately 0.25 mile from your destination you will come upon Worm Creek Springs; from here the trail heads southwest to the lake.

Eastern: Snake River Watersheds

Palisades

Location: Eastern Idaho, 50 miles east of Idaho Falls.
Size: 131,413 acres.
Administration: USDAFS, Targhee National Forest.
Management status: Proposed wilderness.
Ecosystems: Middle Rocky Mountain steppe/coniferous forest/alpine meadow province, characterized by complex and high, steep mountains fed by numerous small feeder springs and alpine lakes; Precambrian granite and sedimentary and volcanic rock; Douglas fir forest type with sagebrush steppe and smaller areas of alpine vegetation.
Elevation range: 5,634 feet at the town of Alpine to 10,025 feet at Mount Baird.
System trails: 256 miles.
Maximum core to perimeter distance: 7 miles.
Activities: Hiking, horseback riding, fishing, and mountain bike riding.
Best months: July, August, and September.
Maps: Thompson Peak-ID; Palisades Peak-ID; Palisades Dam-ID; Mount Baird-ID; Alpine-ID (USGS 1:1,000,000).

OVERVIEW The Palisades Mountain Range lies on the extreme eastern border of Idaho, bordering Wyoming, and is part of the Greater Yellowstone Ecosystem and the Targhee National Forest. This is a dramatic landscape as the thickly wooded mountains rise steeply from the valley floor and also from the very edges of the man-made Palisades Reservoir.

Winters are harsh here, with extremely cold temperatures common and frequent storms that can deposit several feet of snow within hours. High winds accompanying these storms become blizzards and subsequently blow snow into canyons. These deposits of dense snow melt slowly through the hot and dry summer months and serve to feed the area's many streams.

These feeder streams and the high mountain lakes flow into Palisades Reservoir to the east of the Palisades range. The reservoir was created when a dam was built across the Snake River south of the town of Irwin and serves as an important part of the Snake River fishery system. Rainbow, brook, brown, and cutthroat trout thrive in the depths of the reservoir and successfully use its feeder springs and creeks for spawning grounds.

The Palisades Mountains have been inhabited for thousands of years by many bands of Native Americans, primarily the Shoshone and Bannock. These people hunted and fished throughout the Targhee, and evidence of their resi-

26   PALISADES

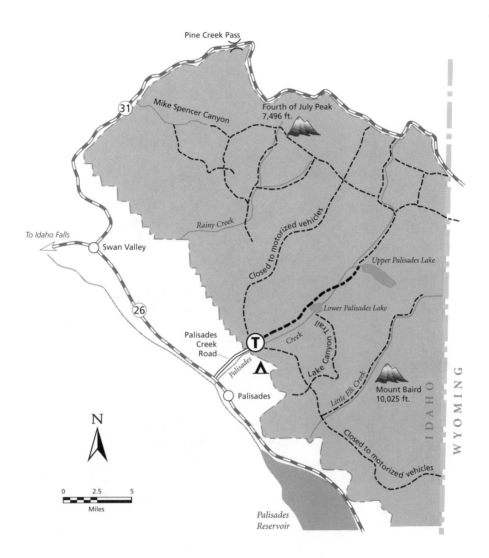

dence can be found in scattered obsidian tailings, places where their craftsmen worked this mineral. These peoples used this hard, sharp material for many tools and also used it as a barter item with other tribes.

The Palisades's abundant streams and steep mountains make this prime habitat for growing herds of bighorn sheep and mountain goat that live above the treeline. The dense brush of the lower elevations provides ample cover and forage for large herds of both elk and mule deer. Moose are commonly seen

The Palisades area is accessed from the South Fork of the Snake River, a renowned fly-fishing river.

feeding along the streams and the shores of the Palisades Reservoir as well as the Snake River. The remarkable abundance of trout in the Snake River has given rise to a thriving population of bald eagles, easily seen in the cotton-woods that line the river.

RECREATIONAL USES The beautiful Palisades Reservoir is a 16,000-acre lake, 16 miles long and up to 3 miles wide. The reservoir is fed by the Snake River to the south at Alpine, Wyoming, and its dam spills out into the South Fork of the Snake River at Palisades, Idaho. The South Fork provides floating and boating opportunities as well as world-renowned fly-fishing.

Late summer berry picking is a popular and productive pastime, and the opportunity to view the fall colors provided by the dense vegetation is an irre-sistible draw to many visitors.

Palisades Reservoir is the focus of most of the outdoor recreation in the Pal-isades Ranger District. The district has provided numerous campgrounds and boating accesses. These amenities have tended to draw users out of the sur-rounding forests and focus them on the reservoir. This redirection of use is very beneficial to the forest as a whole due to the fact that the Palisades Ranger Dis-trict is in close proximity to the ever-growing city of Idaho Falls to the west. The residents of this city, and surrounding towns, prize their outdoor recre-ation and are capable of making a huge impact on forest resources. Some of that impact is also seen in winter when growing numbers of snowmachines make their appearance on area trails. Due to the importance of the Palisades as critical winter range for elk and mule deer, the district has marked and closed many trails to snowmachine traffic.

While thousands of acres adjacent to this land in Wyoming have already been designated as wilderness area, the Idaho side faces much stiffer opposition due to its unique location. The Palisades Ranger District has landed in the middle of a heated controversy between those who lobby for wilderness desig-nation and those who propose multiple use—specifically winter snowmachine use. The area's valuable resources and its location near a major population base will ensure that discussions and studies will continue for the foreseeable future.

HOW TO GET THERE *Palisades Reservoir:* From Idaho Falls take Idaho High-way 26 east 42 miles to Swan Valley. From Swan Valley it is 10 miles to Pal-isades Reservoir.

Palisades Creek: The trailhead is accessed by taking ID 26 7 miles south from Swan Valley to Palisades Creek Road. The turnoff is 3 miles north of the town of Palisades and is fairly well marked. Follow the road approximately 2 miles to the campground and trailhead.

Day Hike

Palisades Creek to Upper Palisades Lake

Distance: 13.5 miles round-trip.
Difficulty: Moderately strenuous.
Topo maps: Thompson Peak-ID; Palisades Peak-ID.

This trail is quite scenic, providing a rare opportunity to view fall foliage displays as well as to experience some truly fine fishing. The best time to take this hike is in early fall when crowds thin out and fall colors have started.

The well-marked trail follows the bottom of the canyon and Palisades Creek as it heads toward the lakes, Lower Palisades Lake and Upper Palisades Lake. Five bridges mark this trail as the route crosses and recrosses the creek. The diversity of the trail's foliage lends itself to a daylong interpretive hike that the district offers in late spring. The Forest Service has left descriptive markers, which are quite interesting, alongside trees, plants, and shrubs in the lower portion of the trail.

Almost 4 miles into the hike you reach the landslide that created Lower Palisades Lake. There is a campsite here as well as the turnoff to Lake Canyon Trail. Stay left as you continue north for another 2 miles where an old Forest Service cabin marks the junction of several other trails. A mile farther will take you to Upper Palisades Lake.

Both Lower and Upper Palisades Lakes have good campsites and great opportunities for fishing for cutthroat trout.

Italian Peaks

27

Location: Idaho–Montana border, 42 miles northwest of Dubois.
Size: 57,742 acres.
Administration: USDAFS, Targhee National Forest.
Management status: Roadless, proposed wilderness.
Ecosystems: Middle Rocky Mountain steppe/coniferous forest/alpine meadow province characterized by complex and high, steep mountains with sharp ridges and cirques; Precambrian granite and sedimentary and volcanic rock; Douglas fir forest type with sagebrush steppe and smaller areas of alpine vegetation; and a complex drainage pattern with numerous intermittent streams.
Elevation range: 8,000 feet at Nicholia to 11,393 feet at Scott Peak.
System trails: 39 miles.
Maximum core to perimeter distance: 6 miles.
Activities: Hiking, backpacking, horseback riding, fishing, and cross-country skiing.
Best months: September, October, and November.
Maps: Morrison Lake-ID/MT; Cottonwood Creek-ID/MT; Eighteenmile Peak-ID/MT; Deadman Lake-ID/MT; Italian Canyon-ID/MT; Scott Peak-ID/MT (USGS 1:1,000,000).

OVERVIEW The Italian Peaks region is a 6-mile-long ridge that runs along the Continental Divide. This mountain range forms part of Idaho's border with Montana. The Italian Peaks rise dramatically from the floor of the Lemhi Valley on the west and are accessed by just a few well-maintained service roads. These roads make sharp switchbacks past old mining sites.

The country here consists primarily of steep, mostly bare, slopes with some short grasses and scattered sagebrush. Isolated stands of aspen and pine lie in sheltered canyons. The lack of vegetation coupled with the extreme elevation gain achieved within a short distance provide outstanding views of the Birch Creek Valley below and the Lemhi Mountain Range to the west.

Wind is the predominant factor here; precipitation is negligible. Winter temperatures can drop below -20 degrees F, and summer will see temperatures above 90 degrees. Due to the weather extremes, the best time for travel here is in the late fall when the daytime temperatures are in the 70s and the nights drop to the 30s. Camping during this season also provides the opportunity to fall asleep to the serenading of the bull elk as they bugle through their mating season.

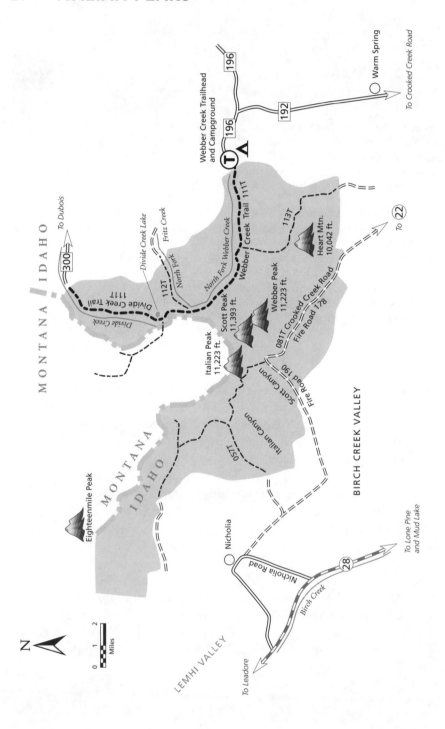

Though one of the least populated regions in the United States today, supporting less than seven people per square mile, the Lemhi Valley was once a hive of activity. By the late 1800s, prospectors had found a wealth of minerals just under the surface of these barren slopes. Hundreds of people moved in and established camps and full-fledged towns in order to extract the precious minerals, which included nickel and silver. This barren landscape readily lent itself to development, as is evidenced by the many primitive access roads built and used by intrepid miners to bring their diggings out to the towns. The quantity and quality of the minerals extracted justified the building of a rail line through the valley, the remains of which can be seen following Idaho Highway 28 on its east side through the length of the valley. Evidence of this extensive mining activity is apparent throughout these mountains but in particular at the ghost town of Nicholia, where scattered tailings, abandoned mines, and bunkhouses now stand silent.

The vast, solitary expanses support large herds of big-game animals including mountain goat at the higher elevations and numerous elk and mule deer farther down. It is not at all uncommon for several different bands of deer to cross the road in front of you as you access these mountains. The desert valley below the Italian Peaks is home to numerous pronghorn antelope and moose and are a common sight along the streambeds.

Of interest in the fall is the spawning of salmon in Birch Creek just south of the town of Lone Pine. Check with the Idaho Department of Fish and Game for the best time to view these fish. Brook and rainbow trout also inhabit these waters and can be fished.

RECREATIONAL USES The aridity and remoteness of this region have aided in keeping the Italian Peaks secluded. The big draw for hikers is stunning views coupled with many natural hot springs.

Archaeological exploration of mining activity from the turn of the twentieth century is also rewarding here. Many old buildings still stand and are well worth visiting, though caution should be exercised while exploring. Many lessons can be learned at these sites, including the utter disregard for the environment or the surrounding natural beauty as evidenced by the old trash piles at the outskirts of many of these ghost towns. A few access roads, which are not maintained, cross the mountains here, some of which are passable in summer and early fall.

The remoteness of the Italian Peaks area has meant that it has not yet been greatly impacted, but its nonwilderness status means that this situation may not last indefinitely.

HOW TO GET THERE *Divide Creek Trail:* From Idaho Falls take I–15 north to Dubois. Turn left (west) on Idaho Highway 22 and drive 18 miles to Warm

Springs/Crooked Creek Road. Turn right and continue 7 miles, where you will bear right at the fork. Five miles down this road you will come to a side road, County Road 192, to Warm Spring. Take this road 12 miles to arrive at the Webber Creek Campground.

Day Hike or Overnighter

Divide Creek Trail

Distance: 15.5 miles one way.
Difficulty: Moderately strenuous.
Topo maps: Deadman Lake-ID; Scott Peak-ID/MT.

This trail offers outstanding and seemingly limitless views of the surrounding countryside and several good soaks in quiet hot springs.

The Webber Creek trailhead offers access to several trails that lead to Italian Peak.

The Divide Creek Trail follows the North Fork of the Webber Creek drainage for 8 miles. This section is an easy walk and the promised hot springs are scattered along here. At this point the trail will Y; turn north to climb for just over 2 miles before arriving at Divide Creek Lake. From Divide Creek Lake the trail follows Divide Creek an additional 5 miles to Forest Road 300.

Lionhead   28

Location: Idaho–Montana border, 12 miles north of Mack's Inn.
Size: 15,014 acres.
Administration: USDAFS, Targhee National Forest.
Management status: Roadless, proposed wilderness.
Ecosystems: Middle Rocky Mountain coniferous forest/alpine meadow province,
Yellowstone Highlands section, characterized by high, glaciated mountains with cirques and
moraines; Precambrian metamorphic and Tertiary volcanic rock; Douglas fir and western
spruce-fir forest types; many short, steep streams with lakes at high elevations.
Elevation range: 6,974 feet at Targhee Creek to 10,240 feet at Targhee Peak.
System trails: 10 miles.
Maximum core to perimeter distance: 5 miles.
Activities: Hiking, backpacking, horseback riding, fishing, and cross-country skiing.
Best months: July, August, and September.
Maps: Targhee Peak-ID/MT; Targhee Pass-ID/MT (USGS 1:1,000,000).

OVERVIEW The Lionhead is a thumblike projection of land that juts north-
ward into Montana from the eastern border of Idaho. The entire Lionhead area
is roughly encircled by Montana's many-armed Hebgen Lake on the north and
east and Idaho's box-shaped Henry's Lake on the south. Yellowstone National
Park lies a mere 8 miles to the east, and Montana's Missouri Flats form the
area's western most border. This area is quite rugged, with very steep and heavily forested slopes rising from the lakes on the valley floors and no road access
into them from the Idaho section. The northern portion from Hebgen Lake
does have several good access roads.

The Lionhead area forms the sharp-edged northern border of the Island
Park caldera, a relatively flat section of country that was created when a prehistoric volcano erupted at this spot. The upper part of the crater blew apart
or collapsed, forming the expanse that extends from Henry's Lake 30 miles
south to Mesa Falls. The Island Park caldera is part of the Yellowstone geo-
thermic area, an area that is continuously in flux and still quite active.

The Lionhead area receives ample winter precipitation in the form of heavy
snowfall; temperatures can drop to -30 degrees F quite easily. The economy in
this area revolves around recreation, and winter snowmachining is not only big
business but virtually the *only* business. Luckily, however, snowmachine users

28   LIONHEAD

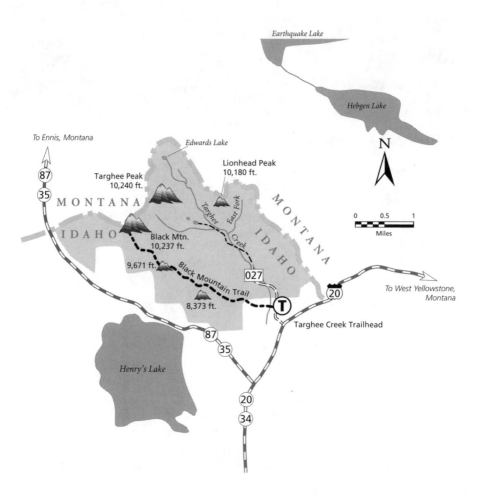

prefer relatively flat tracts of land—the type that exists in abundance within the Island Park caldera. That circumstance, coupled with the ruggedness of Lionhead, serves to largely protect it from winter snowmachine encroachment.

The rugged topography of Lionhead and the contrasting features of the neighboring caldera have also served to protect it from logging interests. The caldera's uniquely flat expanse, heavily carpeted with pine trees, made it a perfect target for logging. Huge amounts of lumber have been harvested here through the years, and the timber companies have replanted the trees in stages within the clear-cuts. Signs along Idaho Highway 34 chronicle the progression of the new growth. With such huge amounts of easily accessible timber, Lionhead has drawn little commercial interest.

High precipitation has fueled the growth of these forests and provided for canyons that are virtually impassable due to the thick vegetation on the mountain floor. These factors help to preserve the plentiful elk and deer herds that inhabit this area. Bighorn sheep enjoy the higher reaches of this country, and grizzly bears have also made this dense habitat their home.

A chain of small lakes exists in the northern section of the Idaho portion of Lionhead, and numerous streams and creeks are interspersed throughout the area, feeding into Hebgen and Henry's Lakes.

RECREATIONAL USES Due to the ruggedness of the country, hiking or horseback riding is the best way to access this area. Camping opportunities at the numerous small backcountry lakes are very rewarding. Native trout abound in these waters, and the solitude of the country is priceless.

Fall is the busiest season as hunters try for the plentiful big game and an opportunity for trophy-size elk and deer. Though the game are large and plentiful, road access is poor, and the dense underbrush makes the hunt quite difficult. As with winter snowmachine use, most users prefer to travel within the milder, less rugged terrain around Island Park, thus helping to preserve the isolation and beauty of the Lionhead area.

The abundant snowfall is extremely attractive to cross-country skiers, but once again the area's landscape allows little access. The best opportunity for cross-country skiing lies at the Targhee Creek Trail, accessed from U.S. Highway 20, 2.5 miles from the junction with Idaho Highway 87.

Fishing is king in this area and is mainly focused on the two large lakes framing Lionhead. To the south lies the large and relatively shallow Henry's Lake, which supports a fish hatchery and a state park on its southern border. Record-size wild cutthroat trout, rainbow-cutthroat hybrids, and brook trout are routinely caught in its waters. Hebgen Lake to the north is a much larger lake with two "fingers" extending toward Yellowstone Park and another extending northwest, for a total length of more than 20 miles. The northwest finger points to Earthquake Lake, the site of a tragic earthquake that occurred in 1959 and claimed the lives of several sleeping campers. Submerged trees are still visible beneath the surface of the water, and the interpretive center is well worth a stop. Fly-fishing for rainbow and brown trout is very rewarding throughout this water system.

HOW TO GET THERE *Black Mountain:* From Mack's Inn drive 12 miles north on Idaho Highway 34 to the Targhee Creek Trail turnoff. The Black Mountain Trail takes off from the Targhee Creek trailhead.

Day Hike

Black Mountain

Distance: 12 miles round-trip.
Difficulty: Easy to moderate.
Topo map: Targhee Peak-ID/MT.

This hike offers one of the best views of Henry's Lake to the south as well as some solitary fishing at a small lake near the summit.

The Black Mountain Trail takes off from the Targhee Creek trailhead and bears to the left. The trail climbs gradually as it follows the canyon made by Targhee Creek, and passes the dramatic Targhee Peak on the right and then ascends to Black Mountain. The trail disappears before the summit, but picking a path is not difficult. At 10,237 feet, Black Mountain provides an excellent vantage point to Idaho, Montana, and Henry's Lake.

Anderson/Allen/West Big Holes 29

Location: Idaho–Montana border, 24 miles north of North Fork.
Size: 18,120 acres, Anderson; 50,981 acres, Allen; 81,068 acres, West Big Holes.
Administration: Anderson and Allen: USDAFS, Bitterroot and Salmon National Forests;
West Big Holes: USDAFS, Salmon National Forest.
Management status: Roadless, nonwilderness.
Ecosystems: *Allen and Anderson:* Middle Rocky Mountain coniferous forest/alpine meadow
province, Idaho Batholith section, characterized by moderately glaciated mountains and large
U-shaped valleys; Lower Tertiary and Mesozoic granite; Douglas fir and western ponderosa
forest types. *West Big Holes:* Middle Rocky Mountain coniferous forest/alpine meadow
province characterized by complex and high, steep, strongly glaciated mountains with sharp
alpine ridges and cirques; Precambrian granite; Douglas fir forest type with sagebrush steppe
and smaller areas of alpine vegetation.
Elevation range: 8,080 feet at the Corral Creek trailhead to 9,154 feet at Anderson
Mountain.
System trails: 30 miles.
Maximum core to perimeter distance: 3 miles.
Activities: Hiking, backpacking, horseback riding, cross-country skiing, fishing, and mountain
bike riding.
Best months: July, August, and September.
Maps: Overwhich Falls-ID/MT; Lost Trail Pass-ID/MT; Henderson Ridge-ID/MT; Allan Mtn.-
ID/MT; Shoup-ID/MT; Big Hole Pass-ID/MT; Jumbo Mtn.-ID/MT; Homer Youngs Peak-ID/MT;
Bohannon Spring-ID/MT; Goldstone Pass-ID/MT (USGS 1:1,000,000).

OVERVIEW These mountains form the border of Idaho and Montana in a
narrow strip north and east of Salmon and are a part of the Bitterroot Mountains in the Beaverhead Range extending north into Montana. The Idaho side
of this range is very dry and is characterized by sagebrush hills leading up to
rugged, forested mountains on the Continental Divide. Due to the aridity of
the area there is very little underbrush; however, there are numerous creeks that
make their way south to meet with the Main Salmon River.

The main fork of the Salmon River lies directly south of this range, and
Shoup Road, running east to west, follows it. Numerous forest roads run off
of this road and in toward the Allen, Anderson, and Big Holes. From these
feeder roads several good trails extend farther back into the roadless area.

29A   ANDERSON/ALLEN/WEST BIG HOLES (NORTH SECTION)

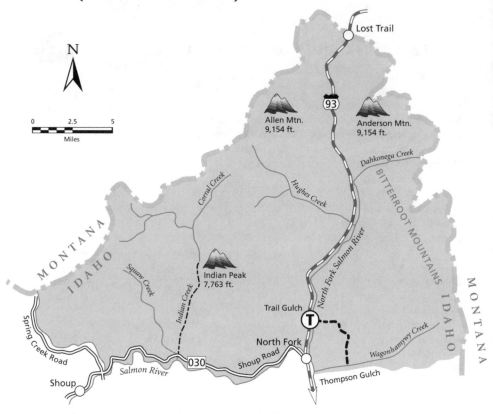

Wildlife is plentiful and includes deer, elk, antelope, black bear, moose, and mountain lion. Bighorn sheep and mountain goats can be found throughout the high country along the divide and are also frequently viewed on the cliff sides adjacent to the Salmon River. Several species of trout live in the streams and lakes, and Chinook salmon and steelhead trout head to the Salmon River and its numerous tributaries in the fall to spawn.

Birds are also quite evident in the area and include several species of grouse, chukar, and one bird that was named after the famous explorers Lewis and Clark: the Clark's Nutcracker.

The exploration party of Lewis and Clark looked at this region and, taking the sage advice of the Lemhi tribe that was with them, concluded that the area was impassable. They subsequently backtracked and found an alternate route to the Pacific Ocean. The trail they followed on this reconnaissance mission can be accessed by walking approximately 2 miles up Wagonhammer Creek to

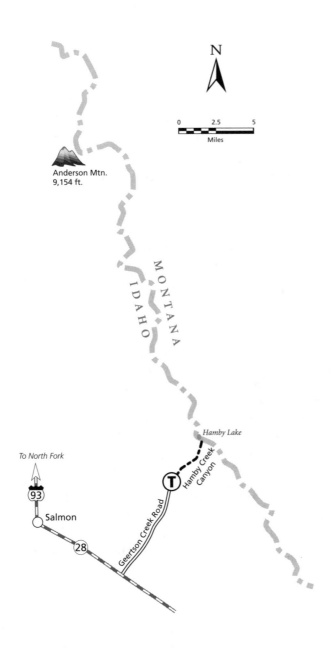

the mouth of Thompson Gulch. The trail here is clearly marked and travels 6 miles to the North Fork of the Salmon River at Trail Gulch. (See the Introduction and chapter 24, "Lemhi Mountains," for more information about the impact these explorers had on Idaho.)

This region has been inhabited for more than 8,000 years; ancestors of the modern Shoshoni-Bannock tribes lived here and left their mark by painting pictographs on exposed rock faces. A particular band of this tribe was nicknamed "the Sheepeaters"—for their habit of hunting and eating bighorn sheep—by settlers. Miners eventually followed the settlers as discoveries of gold were made in the area. Evidence of their activities abounds, including mounds of tailings clogging narrow canyons and abandoned mines and shacks in seemingly inaccessible locations.

RECREATIONAL USES This area is busiest in the fall when visitors and locals alike pursue elk and deer. Hunters gain access by the few primitive forest routes, many of which require four-wheel-drive vehicles. The country becomes even more rugged as you travel farther in, and though the Allen, Anderson, and Big Holes are not designated as wilderness, hiking in from these points will provide true seclusion, as the vast majority of hunters prefer easier access.

The aridity of the area and lack of significant underbrush guarantees a great hiking experience. Deer and bighorn sheep are frequently seen, and hikers are sure to see numerous grouse throughout the day. Fishing can be very rewarding with native trout and arctic grayling lying within the many streams.

Moderate accumulations of snow at lower elevations provide for some great cross-country skiing. Skiers can access the backcountry by skiing the forest routes or by heading out from the Lost Trail Ski Area located 23 miles north of the town of North Fork.

The minerals that brought commerce to this area are still evident in the backcountry, and petrified wood, agate, gold, and opal can still be discovered. Several establishments on the major routes, including Shoup Road, offer on-site collecting for a fee.

HOW TO GET THERE *Hamby Lake:* From Salmon take Idaho Highway 28 south for 7 miles to Geertson Creek Road. The first 4 miles of this road are well maintained, then it changes to a rough road that climbs 7 more miles up a canyon to just below the divide. The hike to Hamby Lake starts here.

Day Hike

Hamby Lake

Distance: 4 miles round-trip.
Difficulty: Moderately strenuous.
Topo map: Bohannon Spring-ID/MT.

This short little hike provides a view into Idaho and Montana as well as the opportunity to fish for native trout.

Geerston Creek Road brings you to just below a saddle of the Continental Divide. From here the trail is a precipitous 1-mile hike to that saddle, and then it climbs an additional mile up and over the divide and down into the start of Hamby Creek Canyon. Hamby Creek Canyon and the nearby Hamby Lake both lie in Montana.

Centennial Mountains   30

Location: Eastern Idaho, 10 miles west of Island Park.
Size: 44,000 acres.
Administration: USDAFS, Targhee National Forest.
Management status: Roadless, nonwilderness.
Ecosystems: Middle Rocky Mountain steppe/coniferous forest/alpine meadow province characterized by complex and high, steep mountains with rounded to sharp ridges and cirques; Precambrian granite and sedimentary and volcanic rock; lake, marsh, and wetlands system bounded by sagebrush steppe; Douglas fir forest type; sizable areas of alpine vegetation; complex drainage pattern with numerous perennial and intermittent streams.
Elevation range: 7,714 feet at West Dry Creek to 9,866 feet at Sawtel Peak.
System trails: 12 miles.
Maximum core to perimeter distance: 4 miles.
Activities: Hiking, backpacking, horseback riding, fishing, cross-country skiing, and wildlife viewing.
Best months: July, August, and September.
Maps: Slide Mtn.-ID/MT; Upper Red Rock Lake-ID/MT; Mt. Jefferson-ID/MT; Sawtell Peak-ID/MT (USGS 1:1,000,000).

OVERVIEW The Centennial Mountains, an arid range, straddle the Idaho/Montana border and form the Continental Divide on Idaho's northeastern corner. The area is small but very important as the waters from these creeks and streams feed directly into the Island Park Reservoir to the south.

The Island Park Reservoir is a shallow, man-made lake that is fed on the north by the Henry's Fork of the Snake River and on the northwest by the many small streams and springs of the Centennial Mountains. It is primarily a rainbow trout fishery with some brook and cutthroat trout included. The fish bred in these waters are subsequently transplanted all over the state. Kokanee salmon are native to the area and spawn in the small streams above the reservoir. The salmon migrate to the lake and reach full maturity there before making the trip back upstream to spawn.

The ruggedness of the Centennials provides habitat for a large number of elk and deer. Harriman State Park, a 16,000-acre refuge located to the northwest of the Centennials, was so designated in order to provide much needed protection for such species as moose, elk, deer, and a wide variety of waterfowl, including the trumpeter swan.

30A CENTENNIAL MOUNTAINS (WEST SECTION)

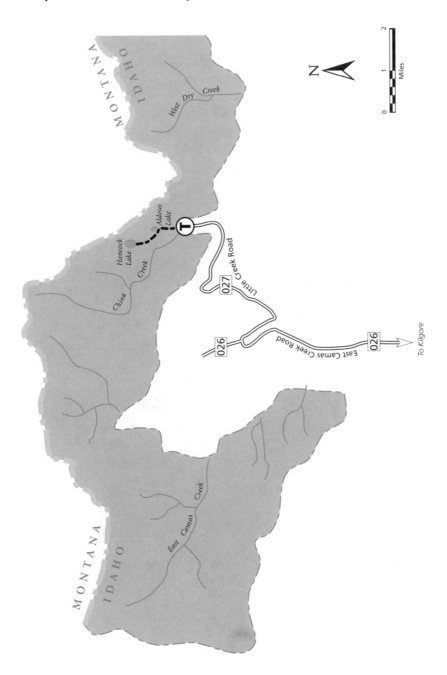

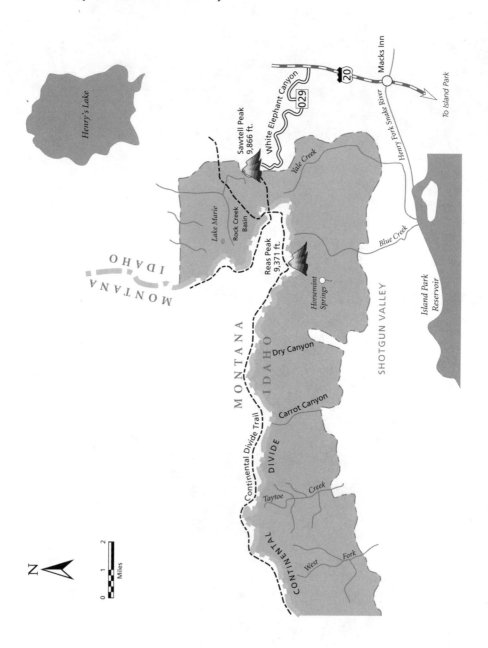

The waters originating in the Centennial Mountains feed the crucial trout fishery of Island Park Reservoir.

The Centennials are also home to the wolverine, an aggressive bearlike mammal that is very rare in Idaho. Wolverines may also be found in the Sawtooth Range near the town of Stanley.

RECREATIONAL USES The Centennials are especially noted for big-game hunting. Due to the rugged landscape, elk, deer, and moose find excellent cover and adequate forage and so are quite plentiful here.

There are quite a few forest access roads; however, most traffic is limited to the fall months when hunters are about. Winter snowmachine use is also a factor. For the most part, though, the Centennials do not receive many visitors as the vast, flat expanses surrounding Island Park offer better sledding.

The Centennials are a part of the Continental Divide, and the Continental Divide Trail bisects its entire length. The view of the nearby lakes and reservoirs from the Centennial section of the trail are clear and fantastic.

Winter brings huge accumulations of snow to these mountains, thus cross-country skiing here is very rewarding. Groomed trails are available in the Shotgun Valley, which lies between the mountains and the reservoir, but they may also be in use by snowmachines. Much more rewarding skiing is available by heading up into the mountains on either access roads closed to vehicles in the winter or on area trails.

Fishing is quite popular here, particularly in the Island Park Reservoir and the Henry's Fork of the Snake River. Yale Creek is a particularly good spot to fish for trout.

HOW TO GET THERE *Aldous and Hancock Lakes:* From Kilgore take East Camas Creek Road (Forest Road 026) north 7 miles until the road Ts. You take the right turn on Little Creek Road (Forest Road 027) and travel for another 6 miles to the Aldous Lake trailhead.

Day Hike

Aldous and Hancock Lakes

Distance: 4 miles round-trip.
Difficulty: Easy.
Topo map: Kilgore-ID/MT.

This trail is out of the way and so makes for a great hike and some great camping at two very nice lakes.

The trail starts at the parking lot and follows China Creek upstream for 0.5 mile before the creek branches. You follow the trail along the right branch for about 1 mile to Aldous Lake. Traveling an additional 1 mile farther along the trail, you will arrive at Hancock Lake.

Both of these lakes have good populations of brook and rainbow trout, and campsites can be made along the shores.

Winegar Hole 31

Location: Eastern Idaho, 18 miles east of Ashton.
Size: 3,247 acres.
Administration: USDAFS, Targhee National Forest.
Management status: Proposed wilderness.
Ecosystems: Northern Rocky Mountain coniferous forest/alpine meadow province characterized by glaciated mountains with moraines; Precambrian metasedimentary rock; lodgepole pine type; lake and marsh with numerous streams.
Elevation range: Relatively flat, averaging 6,300 feet.
System trails: No designated trails.
Maximum core to perimeter distance: 3 miles.
Activities: Photography and nature viewing.
Best months: September and October.
Maps: Porcupine Lake-ID; Indian Lake-ID/WY (USGS 1:1,000,000).

OVERVIEW The 11,000-acre Winegar Hole Wilderness resides solely in Wyoming, but the state of Idaho is strongly considering designating more than 3,000 acres on its side of the border to complement it. This land lies directly south of Yellowstone National Park and is quite a unique wetlands, with tiny lakes and numerous streams patched together with thick marshland. The Idaho portion of the Winegar Hole area follows the Fall River west out of Wyoming. The entire area is remote and very wet and is heavily populated with bear—both black and grizzly—moose, and elk.

Wildlife definitely outnumbers human visitors in Winegar Hole, and therein lies the attraction. Impressive numbers of waterfowl live here along with loons, whooping cranes, and many species of ducks, all feeding off the rich vegetation and insect life spawned by the wet conditions.

RECREATIONAL USES There are very few trails in this area, so exploring should be done with extreme caution and respect.

If you want to see wildlife, this is the place to be. Loons emitting their mournful cries glide over lakes, and bears are sure to enter camp each morning. Finding a dry campsite is a little harder than finding wildlife, although there are campsites near some of the more accessible lakes, and these make good starting points from which to explore. Because animals are so plentiful here it is essential to keep an immaculate camp and to use bear-proof containers for all food storage.

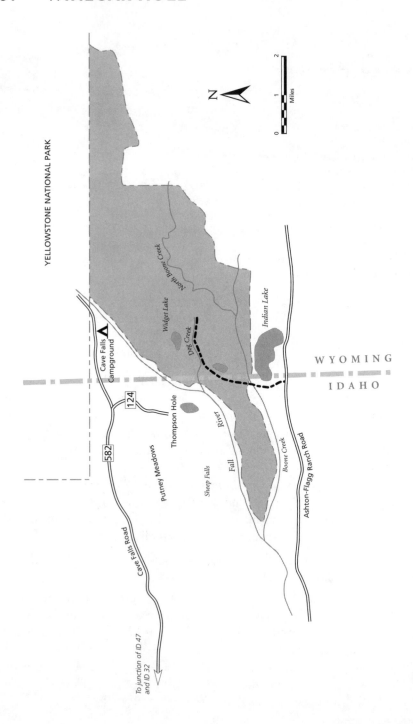

Insects love this country, and the mosquitoes can eat you alive in the spring and summer. The fall season not only mitigates this hazard but brings out the elk herds, which become more active during these months.

HOW TO GET THERE *Indian Lake to Dog Creek and Beyond:* From Ashton take Idaho Highway 47 east to the junction of Idaho Highway 32. Turn right, south, for one mile and turn left on the Ashton–Flagg Ranch Road. The trail starts from a pull-off on the road about 0.5 mile before you see a small lake on your left and the bigger Indian Lake also on your left.

Day Trip

Indian Lake to Dog Creek and Beyond

Distance: 9 miles round-trip.
Difficulty: Easy.
Topo maps: Porcupine Lake-ID; Indian Lake-ID/WY.

This is one of very few trails in the area and a great way to safely view the incredible abundance of wildlife. There are numerous fish in these waters, but most are immature, and the profusion of vegetation makes them hard to access. Exploring near the banks, you will easily find numerous tiny shrimp.

The trail starts off outside the proposed area near Indian Lake. This is a fantastic lake with many loons, ducks, and cranes visible feeding along the shoreline. The trail heads north into Winegar Hole, where the trail crosses Boone Creek as it enters Indian Lake. Traveling on, you will pass another small lake on the right before reaching Dog Creek. You cross Dog Creek here and follow it upstream for 1.5 miles before ending your hike at yet another exquisite tiny lake.

Yellowstone National Park

32

Location: Eastern Idaho, 20 miles west of Ashton.
Size: 158,697 acres in Idaho, 2,221,773 acres total.
Administration: National Park Service.
Management status: Wilderness.
Ecosystems: Northern Rocky Mountain coniferous forest/alpine meadow province characterized by glaciated mountains with moraines; Precambrian metasedimentary rock; lodgepole pine type; lake and marsh with numerous streams.
Elevation range: 5,282 feet at Reese Creek to 11,358 feet at Eagle Peak, averaging between 6,700 feet and 7,840 feet in the predominantly flat Idaho portion.
System trails: No designated trails in the Idaho portion.
Maximum core to perimeter distance: 4 miles.
Activities: Hiking, fishing, and photography.
Best months: September, October, and November.
Maps: Jack Straw Basin-ID/MT/WY; Buffalo Lake NE-ID/MT/WY; Buffalo Lake-ID/WY; Bechler Falls-ID/WY (USGS 1:1,000,000).

OVERVIEW The southwestern corner of Yellowstone National Park, the crown jewel of the National Park system, is anchored in Idaho. This isolated and neglected corner includes some of the least-traveled and secluded terrain in this heavily visited park.

More than three million visitors per year enter Yellowstone National Park to view outstanding natural features such as Old Faithful, the Grand Canyon of the Yellowstone River, and Yellowstone Lake. These tourists enter primarily through the major gateways on the park's four sides. Most of these visitors stick to the main routes and do not venture much beyond the primary attractions. In fact, the Park Service has done a good job of directing visitors by building parking lots and walkways to these sites. This means that despite the huge number of people entering the park, more than 90 percent of these lands remain true wilderness—lands where people are seldom, if ever, encountered. One of the purest of these sections of the park is located in Idaho's portion of Yellowstone National Park.

Archaeological evidence points to the fact that the area has been inhabited for the past 11,000 years. Yellowstone National Park was established as America's first national park in 1872. This act of Congress declared Yellowstone "dedicated and set apart as a public park or pleasuring ground for the benefit

32 YELLOWSTONE NATIONAL PARK

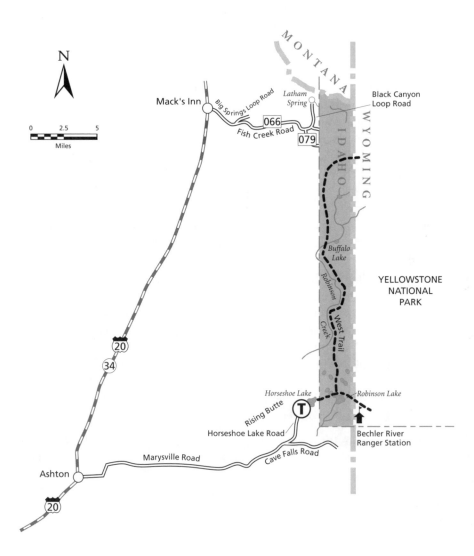

and enjoyment of the people" and "for the preservation, from injury or spoilation, of all timber, mineral deposits, natural curiosities, or wonders . . . and their retention in their natural condition."

Yellowstone's weather is notoriously harsh, but the southwestern corner is unusually moist, even by the park's standard. Heavy winter snow accumulations and numerous streams and marshes make this a haven for many animal species. Grizzly and black bear, bison, elk, and deer are commonly seen throughout the park system. Coyotes are native, and the gray wolf has been reintroduced to Yellowstone National Park as of 1995. The gray wolf was reintroduced with the consensus that not only had they been previous residents of the park but that the renewed presence of this predator would help to balance the herds of large game animals in the ecosystem.

RECREATIONAL USES This is an area of strict solitude as virtually nobody considers it an entrance to Yellowstone National Park. A few local anglers will make an appearance at Horseshoe Lake for the chance at arctic grayling, but otherwise the area remains quiet. Hunting for the plentiful moose, elk, and deer in this corner of Idaho is focused farther south. The proximity of the park, where stiff fines are incurred for even inadvertent hunting infractions, means that hunters actively try to avoid stepping foot within its boundaries.

The chance for solitude and the opportunity to watch wildlife are the prime draws in this corner of Yellowstone, as numerous waterfowl gather here to feed on the fingerling trout and tiny shrimp produced in the lakes and marshes. In turn, these fish feed on the huge insect hatches that the marshes encourage. Fishing is excellent in the many small lakes; however, they do not reach significant size.

Early season cross-country skiing is best experienced in the northern part of Idaho's park due to the drier conditions found there. From Mack's Inn take Big Springs Loop Road 2.5 miles to Fish Creek Road. Follow this road 10 miles to Latham Spring. Continue for 1 mile past the spring, turn right on Forest Road 079, and travel 2 miles. This road will head straight east and dead-end at a spring. On the other side of the spring is Yellowstone National Park's limitless expanses of untracked powder.

HOW TO GET THERE *Horseshoe Lake:* From Ashton take Marysville Road east for 12 miles to the ranger station and the junction with Cave Falls Road. Follow this road 4 miles to Horseshoe Lake Road, which will angle off the main road heading north. Continue on this road for 5 miles until you reach Horseshoe Lake.

Day Hike

Horseshoe Lake

Distance: 3 miles round-trip.
Difficulty: Moderately strenuous.
Topo map: Bechler Falls-ID/WY.

The eastern edge of Horseshoe Lake lies just outside Yellowstone National Park. This lake is a great destination in itself as it is one of the few places where one can fish for native arctic grayling. The marshy country surrounding the lake is also home to a large population of loons, which serenade the camper at sunset.

Compared to what you can expect in the rest of the park, this is not heavily visited country. In fact, Horseshoe Lake remains something of a local's secret, and hiking beyond it will guarantee solitude. Northeast of the lake are numerous smaller lakes, and Robinson Lake lies just past these. This lake also affords exceptional fishing, and there is a trail to it that can be accessed via the Bechler River Ranger Station. The land here is primarily level, but since the ground is marshy and there is no trail access to Robinson Lake from Horseshoe Lake, caution and a good compass are advised when attempting the hike.

Beside being a travel hazard, the wet conditions encourage insects. Traveling in the fall will help alleviate some of this problem. Another hazard: numerous bears that visit the campsites each morning. Remember to bear-proof all food containers and exercise extra caution in the backcountry.

APPENDIX A

Recommended Equipment List

CORE ESSENTIALS FOR DAY TRIPS:

Gear/Accessories
- day pack or "day-and-a-half" climbing-style pack
- water bottle (filled, 1–2 liter capacity)
- matches in a waterproof case/fire starter
- small first aid kit
- pocket knife
- mirror (for emergency signaling)
- whistle
- compass (adjusted for magnetic declination)
- area topo map(s)
- sunscreen
- knife

Clothing
- sturdy, well-broken-in boots (normally light-to-medium weight)
- shirt, sweater, pants, and jacket suited to the season
- socks: wool outer; light cotton, polypro, or nylon inner
- rain gear that can double as wind protection (Gore-tex brand fabric or 60–40 parka and/or rain suit with pants or chaps)
- ski-type hat (balaclava, headband, or stocking cap)
- hat with brim (for sun protection)
- belt and/or suspenders

If You're Staying Over for One Night or Longer, Add the Following:

Gear/Accessories
- backpack/pack cover/extra set of pack straps (internal or external frame is a matter of personal preference)
- tent with fly and repair kit (including ripstop tape)
- sleeping bag (rated to at least 10 degrees F or as season requires)
- sleeping pad (self-inflating type is best)
- stove/fuel bottle (filled), repair kit (including cleaning wire)
- flashlight with extra batteries and bulbs
- candle lantern with spare candle

- cook kit/pot gripper/cleaning pad
- eating utensils: bowl (12–15 oz. with cover), cup, fork, and spoon
- several small drawstring grab bags for miscellaneous items
- trowel
- toilet paper in plastic bag
- biodegradable soap and small towel
- plastic bags (including a large garbage bag) with ties
- toothbrush/ toothpaste/dental floss
- drugs: prescriptions and antibiotics
- sunglasses
- zinc oxide (for sunburn)
- lip balm with sunblock
- eye drops
- aspirin or ibuprofen
- throat lozenges
- laxative
- anti-diarrhea medicine
- decongestant
- antacid tablets
- salt tablets
- scissors/safety pins/small sewing kit
- moleskin (before the blister), second skin (after the blister)
- extra bandages
- insect repellent (spring–summer trips)
- water filter designed and approved for backcountry use
- sharpening stone
- nylon cord (50' to 100' for hanging food, drying clothes, etc.)
- snakebite kit and beesting kit (over-the-counter antihistamine or epi-nephrine by prescription) as needed for area and season

Clothing
- wading sandals or old running shoes
- hiking shorts/swimsuit (summer)
- gaiters (especially for winter trips)
- undershirt and long johns (polypropylene or apilene)
- extra shirt
- extra socks and underwear (3–5 pairs for a weeklong trip)
- bandanna/handkerchiefs
- lightweight cotton or polypropylene gloves

For winter trips and/or river trips add or substitute:

- internal-frame backpack (lowers the center of gravity for skiing)
- space blanket
- ensolite pad (for insulation against the snow)
- pad for stove
- four-season tent
- sleeping bag rated to at least -20 degrees F (down-filled is best during winter)
- snow shovel
- ski accessories
- avalanche cord
- special ski poles that can be threaded together to probe for avalanche victims
- transceivers (at least two in the party)
- warm, waterproof clothing that can be layered
- waterproof bag with additional clothing

Optional for any day or overnight trip:
- compact binoculars
- camera/film/lens brush and paper
- notebook and pencils
- book
- field guides
- fishing tackle (flies and/or spinning gear)

This listing makes a very portable eighty pounds of lightweight gear. Depending on the length and duration of your trip, you can safely manage to reduce the load to thirty-five to fifty pounds. Your pack will weigh eight to ten pounds more during winter with four-season gear and heavier clothing.

APPENDIX B

Conservation Groups in Idaho

Idaho Conservation League
P.O. Box 844
Boise, ID 83701
(208) 345–6933
Fax: (208) 344–0344

The Wilderness Society
1615 M Street, NW
Washington, DC 20096
(800) The–Wild

Sportsmen's Heritage Defense Fund
P.O. Box 1399
Meridian, ID 83680
(208) 888–7020

Idaho Steelhead & Salmon Unlimited
P.O. Box 2294
Boise, ID 83701
(208) 345–4438

Wolf Recovery Foundation
P.O. Box 44236
Boise, ID 83711-0236
(208) 321–0755
E-mail: director@forwolves.org

Henry's Fork Foundation
P.O. Box 852
604 Main Street
Ashton, ID 83420
(208) 652–3567
Fax: (208) 652–3568
E-mail: susans@srv.net

Idaho Environmental Education Association
1910 University Drive
Boise, ID 83725
(208) 385–3490
Fax: (208) 385–4267
E-mail: rmcclosk@bsumail.idbsu.edu

Hornocker Wildlife Institute, Inc.
CEB 319 Blake Street
P.O. Box 3246
University of Idaho
Moscow, ID 83843
(208) 885–6871
Fax: (208) 885–2999
E-mail: hwi@uidaho.edu

Idaho Rivers United
1320 West Franklin
Boise, ID 83702
(800) 574–7481
Fax: (208) 343–9376
E-mail: iru@idahorivers.org

Idaho Watersheds Project
5654 El Gato Lane
Meridian, ID 83642
(208) 888–3293
Fax: (208) 888–0317
E-mail: idwp@poky.srv.net

Sierra Club
85 Second Street, Second Floor
San Francisco, CA 94105-3441
(415) 977–5500
Fax: (415) 977–5799

APPENDIX C

Federal Agencies

The wildland areas covered in this book are administered by one or more of the following agency offices. Check the "Administration" heading in the information block for the area you're interested in, then look below for the address of whom to contact for additional information. For national forest wildlands, the local ranger district office is usually the best source of information on trail conditions, road status, and regulations. The address of each ranger district is listed on the visitor map for each of the national forests in Idaho listed here.

USDA FOREST SERVICE

Idaho Panhandle National Forest
3815 Schreiber Way
Coeur d'Alene, ID 83814
(208) 765–7223

Clearwater National Forest
1273 Highway #12
Orofino, ID 83544
(208) 476–4541

Nez Perce National Forest
Route 2, Box 475
Grangeville, Id 83530
(208) 983–1950

Payette National Forest
106 West Park Street
P.O. Box 1026
McCall, ID 83638
(208) 634–8151

Boise National Forest
1750 Front Street
Boise, ID 83702
(208) 364–4100

Sawtooth National Forest
2647 Kimberly Road East
Twin Falls, ID 83301
(208) 737–3200

Salmon–Challis National Forest
Highway 93 South
P.O. Box 729
Salmon, ID 83467
(208) 756–2215

Caribou National Forest
Federal Building, Suite 282
250 South Fourth Avenue
Pocatello, ID 83201
(208) 236–7500

Targhee National Forest
420 North Bridge Street
P.O. Box 208
St. Anthony, ID 83445
(208) 624–3151

Bitterroot National Forest
1810 North First Street
Hamilton, MT 59840
(406) 363–7117

BUREAU OF LAND MANAGEMENT

Idaho State Office
3380 Americana Terrace
Boise, ID 83706
(208) 384–3000

Boise District Office
3948 Development Avenue
Boise, ID 83705
(208) 384–3300

Burley District Office
15 East 200 South
Burley, ID 83318
(208) 677–6641

Idaho Falls District Office
1405 Hollipart Drive
Idaho Falls, ID 83401
(208) 524–7500

Salmon District Office
P.O. Box 430, Highway 93 South
Salmon, ID 83467
(208) 756–5400

Shoshone District Office
P.O. Box 2-B, 400 West F Street
Shoshone, ID 83352
(208) 886–2206

Coeur d'Alene District Office
1808 North Third Street
Coeur d'Alene, ID 83814
(208) 769–5000

**Snake River Birds of Prey NCA
District Office**
3948 Development Avenue
Boise, ID 83705
(208) 334–9301

Lower Snake River District Office
948 Development Avenue
Boise, ID 83705
(208) 384–3300

Owyhee Field Office
3948 Development Avenue
Boise, ID 83705
(208) 384–3300

**NATIONAL PARK SERVICE,
MONUMENTS, AND RECREATION
AREAS**

**Craters of the Moon National
Monument**
P.O. Box 29
Arco, ID 83213
(208) 527–3257

City of Rocks
P.O. Box 169
Almo, ID 83312
(208) 824–5519

**Hell's Canyon National Recreation
Area**
P.O. Box 832
Riggins, ID 83549
(208) 628–3916

Bruneau Dunes State Park
HC 85, Box 41
Mountain Home, ID 83647
(208) 366–7919

City of Rocks Historical Association
P.O. Box 169
Almo, ID 83312
(208) 824–5519

**Frank Church–River of No Return
Wilderness Area**
Salmon National Forest
P.O. Box 729
Salmon, ID 83467
(208) 756–2215

Selway–Bitterroot Wilderness
Bitterroot National Forest
1810 North First Street
Hamilton, MT 59840
(406) 363–7117

Sawtooth National Recreation Area
Star Route
Idaho Highway 75
Ketchum, ID 83340
(208) 726–8291

Idaho State Department of Parks and Recreation
5657 Warm Springs Avenue
Boise, ID 83712-8752
(208) 334–4199

Idaho Department of Fish and Game
P.O. Box 25
Boise, ID 83707
(208) 334–3700

Yellowstone National Park
Box 168
Yellowstone National Park, WY 82190
(307) 344–7381

MISCELLANEOUS

Idaho Outfitters and Guides Association
P.O. Box 95
Boise, ID 83701
(208) 342–1919

Idaho Department of Commerce
700 West State Streeet
Boise, ID 83720
(800) 635–7820

Idaho Department of Water Resources, Whitewater Recording
1301 North Orchard Street
Boise, ID 83706
(208) 327–7865

Sun Valley Chamber of Commerce
P.O. Box 2420
Sun Valley, ID 83353
(800) 634–3347

APPENDIX D

Topographic Map Lists for Each Area

The descriptions of hikes and river trips in this book are summaries. The intent is to highlight these wild areas and to encourage you to explore them further. In order to adequately prepare yourself for these explorations, you will need two basic types of maps: one or more of the detailed USGS 1:1,000,000-scale topographic (contour) maps listed below; and the Forest Service's national forest visitor map, which is usually 0.5-inch/mile planimetric, and/or the applicable wilderness map, which is on a contour base, or the applicable agency map or guide. At this writing the Forest Service maps cost $3.00, and the USGS topographic maps are $2.50. See Appendix C for where to order the Forest Service maps. If you are ordering more than one map from the Forest Service, it's more efficient to purchase them from the regional office: Information Assistant, USDA Forest Service, P.O. Box 7669, Missoula, MT 59807; (406) 329–3511. USGS maps may be purchased from: Map Distribution, USGS Map Sales, Box 25286, Federal Center, Building 810, Denver, CO 80225.

All of the 1:1,000,000-scale topographic maps presented in this appendix are (2.5-inch/mile) listed line-by-line from right to left beginning on the northern line and ending with the most southeastern map title covering the area.

1. Long Canyon/Selkirk Crest
Shorty Peak-ID, Smith Falls-ID, Smith Peaks-ID, Pyramid Peak-ID, The Wigwams-ID, Roman Nose-ID, Mount Roothaan-ID, Dodge Peak-ID; Kaniska Forest Service Map

2. Salmo–Priest
Continental Mtn.-ID, Grass Mtn.-ID, Upper Priest Lake-ID, Caribou Creek-ID, Priest Lake NW-ID

3. Scotchman Peaks
Trestle Peak-ID, Benning Mtn.-ID/MT, Clark Fork-ID, Scotchman Peak-ID/MT

4. Mallard–Larkins Pioneer Area
Montana Peak-ID, Bathtub Mtn.-ID, Buzzard Roost-ID, Mallard Peak-ID

5. Great Burn
Hoodoo Pass-ID/MT, Straight Peak-ID/MT, Bruin Hill-ID/MT, Schley Mtn.-ID/MT, Rhodes Peak-ID/MT, Granite Pass-ID/MT; 1994 Lolo National Forest Visitor Map

6. City of Rocks
Almo-ID, Cache Peak-ID; City of Rock's Visitors Guide

7. Bruneau Dunes State Park
Bruneau Dunes-ID; Bruneau Dunes Visitor's Map

8. Snake River Birds of Prey National Conservation Area

Coyote Butte-ID, Sinker Butte-ID, Wild Horse Butte-ID, Castle Butte-ID, Jackass Butte-ID, Dorsey Butte-ID, Vinson Wash-ID, Grandview-ID; Snake River Birds of Prey National Recreation Conservation Area, BLM

9. Bruneau–Jarbridge River Area

Hot Spring-ID, Broken Wagon Flat-ID, Crowbar Gulch-ID, Pot Hole Butte-ID, Table Butte-ID, Austin Butte-ID, Winter Camp-ID, Hodge Station-ID, Cave Draw-ID, Stiff Tree Draw-ID, Clover Butte North-ID, Indian Hot Springs-ID, Inside Lakes-ID, Clover Butte South-ID, Triguero Lake-ID, The Arch-ID, Poison Butte-ID, Mosquito Lake Butte-ID, Cowan Reservoir-ID, Dishpan-ID, Murphy Hot Spring-ID; BLM Bruneau-Jarbridge River Guide

10. Owyhee River Canyonlands

Bedstead Ridge-ID, Smith Creek-ID, Castro Table-ID, Dickshooter Reservoir-ID, Frying Pan Basin-ID, Lost Valley-ID, Bull Basin Camp-ID, Red Basin-ID, Brace Flat-ID, Dickshooter Ridge-ID, Battle Creek Lakes-ID, Shoofly Springs-ID, Nichol Flat-ID, Spring Creek Basin-ID, Grassy Ridge-ID, Piute Basin West-ID, Jarvis Pasture-ID, Ross Lake-ID, Flying H Ranch-ID, Star Valley-ID, Coyote Hole-ID, Bull Camp Butte-ID, Four Corners-ID, Juniper Basin-ID, Juniper Basin SE-ID, Mountain View Lake-ID, Three Forks-ID

11. Frank Church–River of No Return Wilderness Area

Boston Mtn.-ID, Spread Creek Point-ID, Sabe Mtn.-ID, Magruder Mtn.-ID, Beaver Jack Mtn.-ID, Nez Perce Peak-ID, Painted Rocks Lake NW-ID, White Water Ranch-ID, Hida Point-ID, Sheep Hill-ID, Dennis Mtn.-ID, Stripe Mtn.-ID, Wood Hump-ID, Blue Joint-ID, Painted Rocks Lake SW-ID, Burgdorf NW-ID, Burgdorf NE-ID, Warren NW-ID, Warren NE-ID, Five Mile Bar-ID, Sheapeater Mtn.-ID, Meadow of Doubt-ID, Arctic Point-ID, Devils Teeth Rapids-ID, Waught Mtn.-ID, Square Top-ID, Horse Creek Butte-ID, Warren SE-ID, Chicken Peak-ID, Mosquito Peak-ID, Lodgepole Creek-ID, Wapiti Creek-ID, Cold Meadows-ID, Cottonwood Butte-ID, Butts Creek Point-ID, Long Tom Mtn.-ID, Shoup SW-ID, Wolf Fang Peak-ID, Big Creek-ID, Bismark Mtn.-ID, Acorn Butte-ID, Vinegar Hill-ID, Papoose Peak-ID, Aggipah Mtn.-ID, Mt. McGuire-ID, Blackbird Mtn. NW-ID, Profile Gap-ID, Center Mtn.-ID, Monument-ID, Mormon Mtn.-ID, Dave Lewis Peak-ID, Pudoin Mtn.-ID, Hoodoo Meadows-ID, Blackbird Mtn.-ID, Yellowpine-ID, Stibnite-ID, Rainbow Peak-ID, Safety Creek-ID, Shellrock Peak-ID, Bear Creek Point-ID, Aparejo Point-ID, Yellowjacket-ID, Chilcoot Peak-ID, Big Chief Creek-ID, Big Baldy-ID, Pungo Mtn.-ID, Norton Ridge-ID, Ramey Hill-ID, Sleeping Deer Mtn.-ID, Meyers Cove-ID, Meyers Cove Point-ID, Chinook Mtn. NW-ID, Chinook Mtn. NE-ID, Greyhound Ridge NW-ID, Greyhound Ridge NE-ID, Sliderock Ridge-ID, Falconberry Peak-ID, Rock Creek-ID, Sheldon Peak-ID, Twin Peaks NW-ID, Chinook Mtn. SW-ID, Chinnok Mtn. SE-ID, Greyhound Ridge SW-ID, Greyhound Ridge SE-ID, Pinyon Peak-ID, Casto-ID, Sherman Peak-ID, Challis Creek Lakes-ID, Twin Peaks SW-ID, Deadwood Res. NE-ID, Bear Valley Mtn.-ID, Blue Bunch Mtn.-ID, Cape Horn Lakes-ID, Langer Peak-ID, Knapp Lakes-ID, Mt. Jordan-ID, Custer-ID.

12. Sawtooth Wilderness

Mt. Cramer-ID, Snowyside Peak-ID, Stanley-ID, Stanley Lake-ID, Warbonnet Peak-ID, Mount Everly-ID, Grandjean-ID, Edaho Mtn.-ID, Nahneke Mtn.-ID, Atlanta West-ID, Atlanta East-ID; 1990 Sawtooth National Recreation Area Visitor Map (includes the Sawtooth Wilderness Area)

13. Selway-Bitterroot Wilderness

Ranger Peak-ID, Savage Ridge-ID, White Sand Lake-ID, Huckleberry Butte-ID, Greenside Butte-ID, Fish Lake-ID, McConnell Mtn.-ID, Hungry Rock-ID, Cedar Ridge-ID, Jeanette Mtn.-ID,

Blodgett Mtn.-ID, Chimney Peak-ID, Fenn Mtn.-ID, Big Rock Mtn.-ID, Shissler Peak-ID, Freeman Peak-ID, Wahoo Peak-ID, Saddle Mtn.-ID, Tenmile Lake-ID, Selway Falls-ID, Fog Mtn.-ID, Mink Peak-ID, Moose Ridge-ID, Dog Creek-ID, Twin Butte-ID, Hunter Peak-ID, El Capitan-ID, Anderson Butte-ID, Vermillion Peak-ID, Running Lake-ID, Wylies Peak-ID, Gardiner Peak-ID, Mount George-ID, Mount Paloma-ID, Tin Cup Lake-ID, Sable Hill-ID, Green Mtn.-ID, Three Prong Mtn.-ID, Spot Mtn.-ID, Burnt Strip Mtn.-ID, Watchtower Peak-ID, Boston Mtn.-ID, Spread Creek Point-ID, Sabe Mtn.-ID, Magruder Mtn.-ID, Beaver Jack Mtn.-ID, Nez Perce Peak-ID, Sheep Hill-ID, Dennis Mtn.-ID, Stripe Mtn.-ID, Wood Hump-ID, Blue Joint-ID

14. Hell's Canyon Wilderness Area
Kirkwood Creek-ID/OR, Lucile-ID, Old Timer Mtn.-ID/OR, Kessler Creek-ID, Squirrel Prairie-ID/OR, He Devil-ID, Heavens Gate-ID, White Monument-ID/OR, Purgatory Saddle-ID

15. Boulder/White Cloud Mountains
Stanley-ID, Casino Bar-ID, Robinson Bar-ID, Livingston Creek-ID, Potaman Creek-ID, Obsidian-ID, Washington Peak-ID, Boulder Chain Lakes-ID, Bowery Creek-ID, Alturas Lake-ID, Horton Peak-ID, Galena Peak-ID, Ryan Peak-ID, Galena-ID, Easley Hot Springs-ID, Amber Lakes-ID

16. Gospel Hump Wilderness
Sawyer Ridge-ID, Sourdough Peak-ID, North Pole-ID, Hanover Mtn.-ID, Marble Butte-ID, Buffalo Hump-ID, Carey Dome-ID, Johnson Butte-ID, Cottontail Point-ID, Florence, Dairy Mtn.-ID, Orogrande-ID, Columbia Ridge-ID, Mackay Bar-ID

17. Meadow Creek
Selway Falls-ID, Fog Mtn.-ID, Anderson Butte-ID, Vermillion Peak-ID, Blackhawk-ID, Sable Hill-ID, Running Lake-ID, Grouse Creek-ID

18. Pioneer/White Knob Mountains
Prophyry Peak-ID, Lehman Butte-ID, Mackay Reservoir-ID, Big Black Dome-ID, Copper Basin Knob-ID, Shelly Mtn.-ID, Big Blind Canyon-ID, Silverspur Ridge-ID, SunValley-ID, Hyndman Peak-ID, Grays Peak-ID, Star Hope Mine-ID, Smiley Mtn.-ID, Miller Peak-ID, Grouse-ID, Appendicitis Hill-ID, Baugh Creek SW-ID, Baugh Creek-ID, Muldoon-ID, Trail Creek-ID, Blizzard Mountain North-ID, Champagne Creek-ID, Seaman's Creek-ID, Wood River Reservoir-ID, Lake Hills-ID, Fish Creek Reservoirs-ID

19. Secesh/Payette Crest
Victor Peak-ID, Loon Lake-ID, Pony Meadows-ID, Pilot Peak-ID, Box Lake-ID, Enos Lake-ID, Fitsum Summit-ID, Fitsum Peak-ID, Paddy Flat-ID, Blackmare-ID

20. Smoky Mountains
Marshall Peak-ID, Frenchman Peak-ID, Galena-ID, Cayuse Point-ID, Ross Peak-ID, Newman Peak-ID, Paradise Peak-ID, Baker Peak-ID, Boardman Peak-ID, Sydney Butte-ID, Dollarhide Mtn.-ID, Buttercup Mtn.-ID

21. Great Rift Backcountry Area
Woodville-ID, Morgans Pasture NE-ID, Nichols Reservoir-ID, Arco South-ID, Inferno Cone-ID, The Watchman-ID, Fingers Butte-ID, Paddleford Flat-ID, Little Park-ID, North Laidlaw Butte-ID, Fissure Butte-ID, Pratt Butte-ID, Pagari Well-ID, Wagon Butte-ID, Laidlaw Butte-ID, Bear Park West-ID, Bear Park East-ID, Black Ridge Crater-ID, Halfway Lake-ID, Laidlaw Lake-ID, Bear Park SW-ID, Mule Butte-ID, Owinza-ID, Senter-ID, Shale Butte-ID, Pillar Butte-ID, Pillar Butte NE-ID, Schoodle Well-ID, Rattlesnake Butte-ID, Pillar Butte SE-ID, Gifford Spring-ID, Register Rock-ID

22. Craters of the Moon National Monument
Inferno Cone-ID, The Watchman-ID; Craters of the Moon Visitor's Map

23. Mount Borah
Grouse Creek Mtn.-ID, Doublespring-ID, Dickey Mtn.-ID, Borah Peak-ID, Burnt Creek-ID, Elkhorn Creek-ID, Leatherman Peak-ID, Massacre Mtn.-ID, Mackay-ID

24. Lemhi Mountains
Allison Peak-ID, Lem Peak-ID, May NW-ID, May NE-ID, Patterson NW-ID, Mat SE-ID, Patterson SW-ID, Patterson SE-ID, Donkey Hills NW-ID, Donkey Hills NE-ID, Gilmore NW-ID, Gilmore NE-ID, Donkey Hills SE-ID, Gilmore SW-ID, Gilmore SE-ID, Nicholia SW-ID, Hawley Mtn. SE-ID, Diamond Peak NW-ID, Diamond Peak NE-ID, Diamond Peak SW-ID, Diamond Peak SE-ID, Eightmile Canyon-ID, Howe NE-ID, Tyler Peak-ID

25. Cache Crest/Mount Naomi
Mink Creek-ID, Paris Peak-ID, Paris-ID, Mapleton-ID, Egan Basin-ID, St. Charles-ID

26. Palisades
Thompson Peak-ID, Palisades Peak-ID, Palisades Dam-ID, Mount Baird-ID, Alpine-ID

27. Italian Peaks
Morrison Lake-ID/MT, Cottonwood Creek-ID/MT, Eighteenmile Peak-ID/MT, Deadman Lake-ID/MT, Italian Canyon-ID/MT, Scott Peak-ID/MT

28. Lionhead
Targhee Peak-ID/MT, Targhee Pass-ID/MT

29. Anderson/Allen/West Bigholes
Overwhich Falls-ID/MT, Lost Trail Pass-ID/MT, Henderson Ridge-ID/MT, Allan Mtn.-ID/MT, Shoup-ID/MT, Big Hole Pass-ID/MT, Jumbo Mtn.-ID/MT, Homer Youngs Peak-ID/MT, Bohannon Spring-ID/MT, Goldstone Pass-ID/MT

30. Centennial Mountains
Slide Mtn.-ID/MT, Upper Red Rock Lake-ID/MT, Mtn. Jefferson-ID/MT, Sawtell Peak-ID/MT

31. Winegar Hole
Porcupine Lake-ID, Indian Lake-ID/WY

32. Yellowstone National Park
Jack Straw Basin-ID/MT/WY, Buffalo Lake NE-ID/MT/WY, Buffalo Lake-ID/WY, Bechler Falls-ID/WY

INDEX

ABOUT THE AUTHOR

Wendy Swope has lived in the "wilds" of the Intermountain West for the past twenty years. Her experiences include living through a Wyoming winter in a tipi with her husband, hiking extensively through Utah's many ranges while working for seismograph companies, and exploring the varied backcountry of Idaho by foot and by water with her husband and five kids.

Swope currently is employed as a registered nurse in the Intensive Care Unit at Eastern Idaho Regional Medical Center.